STOICISM COLLECTION: 2-IN-1 BUNDLE

Stoicism in Modern Life + The Most Inspiring Stoic Quotes - The #1 Beginner's Box Set for Self-Awareness and Mental Toughness in Today's World

STOICISM IN MODERN LIFE

Discover How to Develop Your Self-Awareness, Improve Your Mental Toughness and Self-Discipline in Today's World
(Beginner's Guide)

By Tom Oxford

Congratulations on purchasing Stoicism in Modern Life, thank you for doing so!

This guide on the philosophy of stoicism is going to support you in understanding what stoicism is, how it works, and why it is so imperative to harness stoicism for you to achieve success in your life, both professionally and personally. The ancient art of stoicism is perhaps one of the strongest philosophies that can teach you how to master the art of your mind and start taking control over your life in a powerful and meaningful way.

Thanks again for choosing this audiobook! Every effort was made to ensure it is full of as much useful information as possible. Please enjoy!

Table of Contents

Introduction

Throughout this audiobook, I am going to share with you the best ways that you can harness and develop stoicism and use it in your daily life. From your relationships to your career, you are going to discover just what it takes to really change your life from the inside out and experience massive shifts as a result. I realize that changes are not something that can happen overnight; it happens gradually. But I am confident that if you begin applying the skills that I teach you right here in this very book that you will be able to start experiencing massive transformations quickly. As you continue applying these skill, you will continue to experience greater changes and transformations as you grow through life with the inner strength needed to overcome anything that you may have to face.

I encourage you to realize that your transformation is going to come from two significant places: understanding and consistency. Make sure that you take the time to fully understand and comprehend the concepts that I am sharing with you and that they make sense to you as you listen through this audiobook. That way, when it comes to discovering how you can apply these very techniques into your own life, you can do so in a complete and well-rounded manner. Once you have discovered exactly how to apply them, you are going to need to apply them consistently so that you can continue experiencing changes. As they say, "Rome wasn't built in a day, but they were laying bricks every hour." Change is not something that is achieved in one leap, but as long as you continue working towards your desires, then plenty can be accomplished.

You may be wondering what stoicism is exactly. Perhaps you have heard of the term a few times before but you weren't clear on what it was, or maybe this is your first time hearing it and you have never even considered that it might be a thing. So, before we dive in, I want to make sure that you have a clear understanding of just what it is that you are about to learn for the duration of the time that we are going to spend together! After all, your time is important, and you want to make sure that you are investing it into something that is actually going to help you have a major impact on your life.

Stoicism, according to the dictionary, is "the endurance of pain or hardship without a display of feelings and without complaint." On a surface level, this might sound somewhat harsh and outdated since we are currently living amongst a time where emotions are highly praised and are encouraged in most situations. While I am not saying that emotions should ever be discouraged or bottled up, what I am saying is that there is an appropriate manner in which emotions should be handled, especially in certain situations. By learning about stoicism, you develop a sense of emotional intelligence that enables you to both experience and express your emotions while also gaining the benefits of not letting your emotions take over you. Despite stoicism being a form of emotional intelligence, you should realize that this is only one element of what stoicism truly is. This particular philosophy not only educates you on key aspects of emotional intelligence, but also supports you in developing mental toughness, resiliency, and the ability to be more accepting of both yourself and others in your life. By embodying all of these elements of stoicism, you can develop a sense of maturity that supports you in experiencing a fuller life both personally and professionally as you equip yourself with the proper tools to navigate any situation you may face in life.

If you are ready to begin embracing the power of stoicism and learning about how you can develop it and apply it to your own life, then I would say it is time that we begin! Please take a moment to prepare yourself for what might be one of the most life-changing experiences you will ever endure. And, of course, be sure to enjoy!

Chapter 1: Understanding Stoicism

You now have a basic understanding of what stoicism is in regard to it being a form of emotional intelligence and mental resiliency, but you still do not truly understand the full concept of stoicism. Stoicism is a rather complex concept that actually has a rich history in ancient Greece. To truly understand what it is, how it works, and what purpose it is designed to achieve, you need to look at it from the earliest developments of its philosophy. From there, you can begin to understand why this particular skill is so valuable, and how it continues to relate to the modern world even though we have evolved so much from those early days.

In this chapter, we are going to explore important concepts around stoicism, such as its Greek roots and how it relates to modern-day living. You are also going to develop an understanding of what the real goal of stoicism is and why it is actually an incredibly valuable tool despite the fact that it was poorly executed for many years in our recent history. This way, you can understand exactly how stoicism relates to you and why it is such an important concept for you to grasp and comprehend.

Ancient Greek School of Philosophy

Stoicism was originally introduced to society back in the ancient Greek school of philosophy by a gentleman named Zeno of Citium. It was originally founded in c. 300 B.C.E. Inspired by Cynics, Zeno was a disciple of Socrates and spent his life as a philosopher, attempting to understand the purpose of life and the meaning of various human realities and experiences. One of Zeno's most influential followers was named Chrysippus, and it was Chrysippus who was actually responsible for molding the philosophy that is now known as stoicism.

The majority of scholars who educated themselves on Greek philosophy and stoicism typically divided the history of stoicism into three different phases: early Stoa, middle Stoa, and late Stoa. Early Stoa was the initial development of stoicism as founded by Zeno in his school of philosophy. The latter two phases were followed up by both the Greeks and the Romans who continued to try and understand the concepts of stoicism and develop upon it, molding it into modern-day stoicism. It was during the latter phase where Romans truly fostered the idea of stoicism, with some of the Empires praising it and cherishing it and others persecuting it.

Back in these early days, stoicism was a philosophy that was supposed to teach individuals how to develop self-control so that they could overcome destructive emotions. True stoicism was not designed to encourage people to extinguish or ignore their emotions, but instead to discover how they could transform those emotions through the voluntary absence of worldly pleasures, also known as "Asceticism". As an ancient leader, this would mean that you would have the self-control to feel emotions of anger or jealousy without immediately acting upon them so as to seek immediate worldly pleasure through revenge. Instead, one would willingly abstain from the pursuit of pleasure and find a resolution that worked in a less intense or cruel manner.

The usage of stoicism was intended to support a person in developing a clearer sense of judgment, a deeper sense of inner calmness, and the freedom from their suffering. It was not implemented as merely a skill or a belief system but instead was used as a way of life by those who wished to implement it into their daily living habits and rituals. Stoicism, then, was about an ethical way of living that would enable people to experience their emotions without immediately acting upon them in excessive or sometimes animalistic ways. Some argue that it was fundamental in our ability to evolve further as species to be able to live in a more civilized manner amongst other humans.

The Purpose for Stoicism in Society

Stoicism is a rather complex tool that can be used to elevate people out of many varieties of worldly suffering. To get a deeper understanding of how, we are going to look at the many ways that stoicism can help end needless suffering and promote a more positive and healthy society in general. The same concepts that allowed stoicism to be so powerful and helpful back in ancient Greece and Rome are the same reasons as to why it continues to be such a powerful concept in modern society.

Perhaps, one of the biggest benefits ancient civilizations gained from stoicism was the development of emotional intelligence which leads to individuals being able to train themselves into choosing between emotional and rational thought responses. This may have been highly fundamental in our history by preventing humans from having aggressive and violent reactions to their emotions so that they could begin having more intentional and thoughtful responses. For example, say an ancient Greek *archon*, or ruler, had been slighted by someone and experienced an intense burst of anger because he was angry that someone would defy his absolute power. Without stoicism, that ruler may simply sentence the individual to death and have him murdered publicly as a display of absolute power and to warn others off of wronging him. On an individual level, this may lead to deep inner feelings of trauma and guilt, particularly if the *archon* later regretted his decision and wished that he had spared the life of the other individual. This was not an uncommon experience back in the days of ancient Greece, where people would murder just about anyone out of anger, even their loved ones. Obviously, this leads to intense experiences of guilt and shame, and deep feelings of grief and despair which would lead to intense worldly suffering within the person who had experienced the aggressive outrage. With stoicism, the ruler would experience the intense anger but choose to experience it passively, or in a way that allows them to recognize and experience it but not act in such an intense and violent manner. As a result, they would avoid the needless endurance of guilt, shame, grief, and despair at the loss of an individual at their own hand.

While intense violent outbursts are not as common in the modern world, they still can happen from time to time, and they can still have just as negative of an impact on both parties as they ever did. While we do not exercise things like the death penalty or intense violent punishments like we once did, there are still many unkind things that people do as a way to exercise revenge against those who have upset or wronged them. Embodying stoicism can help prevent needless suffering by helping you not have such intense emotional outbursts towards those around you, thus allowing you and the other person to avoid unnecessary feelings of suffering.

Another way that stoicism can avoid feelings of suffering is by teaching a healthy detachment from feelings of loss, lack, or desperation. In both ancient and modern societies, many people have lived in conditions that are often deemed less than ideal by those living in them and by those living around them. Unfortunately, no real solutions have yet been presented to help every person in every society live a comfortable life free of any worldly sufferings such as poverty or hunger. While stoicism cannot earn you a greater income or feed a hungry tummy, it can prevent you from experiencing intense victimhood from these types of worldly experiences. In that detachment, you can see yourself as being separate from your worldly suffering and able to still experience joy and happiness despite the troubles that are happening in your life. This may not be equal to increasing your income or finding food during hungry times, but it can prevent you from experiencing these with the added stress of inner suffering and pain. For some people, the liberation from their own inner suffering is enough for them to find a solution to increase their income or find food to eat.

There are many additional types of worldly sufferings that people may have and have faced throughout the history of humankind. Stoicism may not always be the worldly answer to helping you get your hands on the resources that you need to liberate yourself from challenges, but it can certainly be a powerful tool in helping you prevent additional suffering. As such, stoicism can be a profound way to help you make the best out of any situation and use yourself as your own best tool in helping you to discover and experience a better way of living.

The Goal of Stoicism

The goal of stoicism is ultimately to end the experience of inner suffering by providing individuals with the freedom from passion (or anguish) through the pursuit of reason. By fostering the ability to be objective, unemotional, and mentally clear regarding any worldly challenges that a person may face, they can gain a greater sense of control over their worldly responses and avoid further suffering. So, in a very basic sense, the goal is to end unnecessary inner suffering in individuals through stoicism.

When you choose to embrace stoicism in your own life, your goal is not to experience no suffering at all but to detach from worldly suffering and eliminate the development of unnecessary suffering. So, instead of experiencing a great amount of anger and acting on it, thus also bringing about a great amount of guilt, you would instead experience anger and make the inner choice to experience it passively. Through this passive experience, you can overcome the feelings of guilt and shame and avoid further unnecessary suffering from within.

Of course, developing stoicism is not the easiest and most natural thing in a society that often uses shame and guilt as a way to pressure people into doing certain things throughout their lives. However, learning how to embrace stoicism will allow you to teach yourself to intentionally and willingly step back from the unnecessary suffering of these pressures and begin to take more control over yourself and your inner emotional experiences. This way, you can start experiencing the world around you more objectively and with more control over what your actual experience is, rather than feeling pushed around by the society around you.

Why Stoicism Is Not Emotional Avoidance

In recent Western history, a form of "skill" was being taught that educated people on the importance of avoiding their emotions so that they could go through life without the needless suffering of emotions. In this way, philosophies like stoicism were somewhat extorted to attempt to pressure people into accepting the often unfair realities that were being dealt with them by their superiors. Bosses, for example, would encourage an extorted form of stoicism to their employees to avoid having employees that would complain and attempt to revolt against the system in favor of staying quiet, calm, and compliant. This was taught on such a wide-scale level that to this day, many elders that continue to live in our modern world experience intense challenges when it comes to expressing or experiencing any form of emotion in a positive and healthy manner.

Anytime we discuss something like stoicism, which is the willful abstinence from intense emotional reactions, it is important that we also recognize that it is not about the *avoidance* of emotions altogether. Instead, it is about recognizing and experiencing emotions but intentionally choosing to address them more constructively and productively. This is why stoicism is often related to emotional intelligence: because it supports you in choosing reasonable and rational decisions over emotional ones.

Exercising stoicism in the modern world, free of the exploitation of those who attempted to profit and benefit off of others' complete lack of emotions, does not mean living your life void of emotions. Rather, it means living your life in harmony with your emotions and learning how to exercise them and use them in a way that empowers you but refrains from you making irrational decisions that lead to further suffering later on. In this way, your emotions, which are an important part of your human experience, continue to be honored and valued, but they do not become a hindrance for your ability to experience a positive Earthly life.

How Stoicism Relates to Modern Daily Living

The modern world is heavily driven by stress, which can be filled with unnecessary amounts of pressure and overwhelming emotions. If you live in modern-day society, chances are that you can pick apart many pieces of your daily life that are filled with stress, overwhelming emotions, and pressure from things that are considered normal or standard in modern living. For example, you might find that having to wake up early to go to a career you do not really enjoy can be stressful. Aside from work, there are many other everyday stresses that people face in their lives, too: traffic, not enough time to get everything done, messy homes, overwhelmed schedules, feeling obligated to spend time with people they may not like, and so forth. Many parts of our modern lives are plagued by stress which can lead to emotions like anger, jealousy, resentment, disappointment, guilt, shame, and other painful emotions that resemble suffering.

By learning how to apply stoicism into your everyday life, especially in the modern world, you can learn how to begin experiencing freedom from these types of suffering so that you can enjoy more freedom in your daily life. Through stoicism, you can detach from the feelings of frustration in traffic, stress in going to work, or jealousy in following people on social media who flaunt the things that you wish you had in your own life. You also allow yourself to develop mental toughness and resiliency so that you can face challenging experiences in your life, including challenging emotional experiences, without such intense feelings of suffering attached to your experiences.

As you will learn throughout this audiobook, there are many ways that true stoicism can continue to serve us in our modern world. By embracing these methods and building your mental toughness and your ability to choose reasonable thinking over emotional thinking, you can start making decisions for yourself that will improve your quality of living. As such, your suffering associated with stress and other stress-related emotions will begin to minimize as you begin enjoying a more peaceful and positive life.

Chapter 2: Mental Toughness

The first step in becoming more stoic is learning how to build mental toughness, as mental toughness is a key tool in helping you overcome emotional responses to life. When you develop your mental toughness, you enable yourself to have the mental strength required to recognize emotional experiences and rationally think your way through the process. You also equip yourself with the tool that you need to overcome challenges without feeling defeated and allowing yourself to wallow into a victim mentality.

In this chapter, you are going to begin developing your own mental toughness so that you can begin developing the strength required to navigate challenging situations without feeling so overwhelmed and overcome by emotions. This way, you can start laying the foundation for your own personal ability to detach from challenging emotional situations and choose to passively experience your emotions in a way that reduces your personal suffering. As you go through this chapter, make sure that you understand that developing mental toughness may sound easy on paper, but in all reality, it is not always as easy as it may sound. In a society that is plagued by stress and stress-related emotional struggles, mental illness and mental chaos or overwhelming emotions are extremely common and all of these can lead to it taking longer for you to develop your mental toughness. Realize that your goal here is not to suddenly develop a "thicker skin," but instead to start understanding and enforcing the practices associated with mental toughness so that you can begin seeing results from your practice. If you remain consistent and practice these tools to the best of your ability, then in due time, you will begin experiencing all of the benefits of mental toughness. While it may not be an immediate change of pace, it will be one that is certainly worth your while, and that will pave the way for you to have many more positive experiences going forward.

Why Mental Toughness Matters

When it comes to developing stoicism, or the capacity to approach challenging emotional matters with intention and focus, mental toughness is the foundation of your practice because it equips you with the strength to control your mind. Our minds are incredibly powerful tools that have the capacity to support us or hinder us in achieving the things that we desire in life, depending on how we are using them. Many people never intentionally take control over their minds and live their entire lives being victimized by their mental processes. This often happens because people do not realize that their minds are only working instinctively and with the intention of producing survival: our minds have the capacity to be used for great things, but they do not naturally do so. The people who achieve great things have developed mental toughness by developing and harnessing the tools required to actually take control over their minds and make a difference.

See, the average human mind values pleasure over anything else. Pleasure, or feelings of positive emotions and sensations, gives the mind the belief that we are experiencing something positive and that is friendly to our survival. When we experience something that is not pleasurable, it is not believed to be supportive of our survival, and therefore the mind is either neutral or negative towards it in favor of something more pleasurable. As a result, we will often instinctively behave in ways that please us, even if the acquisition of that pleasure seems strange or uncomfortable in and of itself. A basic example of this is seen with procrastination: often people procrastinate because it is more pleasurable to do nothing or relax than it is to actually engage in the task that they are putting off. Once procrastination begins to produce stress, it stops becoming pleasurable, so the person jumps into the task and tries to accomplish it rapidly to eliminate the stress and come back to the point of pure pleasure.

The problem with the human mind favoring pure pleasure is that it can be so sneaky in how it works on a subconscious level that many people have no idea what is actually driving their pleasure-seeking behaviors. To them, their behaviors may be normal or natural, and the belief that anything should be done in any other way is unnatural and uncomfortable. They may begin to produce mental beliefs or protests to justify why *they* are incapable of changing their ways when really it is just their human mind attempting to protect its access to pleasure.

When you develop mental toughness, you learn how to put off pleasure by delaying gratification through mental skills that allow you to see the benefits in doing so. These skills are developed in a way that allows you to take control over your mind and consciously control the way that pleasure is acquired so that you are not acquiring it through ways that actually increases displeasure later on. You do so by developing tools that are capable of increasing your conscious control over your mind, such as clarity, the ability to be unbiased, the capacity to exercise rational thinking, and mental resiliency. The more you develop these skills, the stronger they become and the easier it is for you to rely on them even when times are challenging. As a result, you are able to experience greater mental toughness which will pave the way for the rest of your development of stoicism.

Developing Your Mental Clarity

The first step in developing mental toughness is developing your mental clarity, which essentially means building your self-awareness and learning how to consciously recognize behaviors that you may have. When you experience mental clarity, your capacity to have a clear understanding of your emotions, your thoughts, and the stimuli that trigger all of these experiences is increased. It becomes easier for you to understand yourself and comprehend both your instinctive responses and your rational responses because you are able to see yourself through a clearer lens.

When you experience mental clarity, you are experiencing life through mental alertness that free of stress. Because it is stress-free, you can see things as they are, rather than through your own inner perceptions that may result in you shaping the world around you in an unrealistic manner. As a result, mental clarity will also help you establish things like the ability to be unbiased or to rationally respond to situations without being hijacked by your emotions.

You develop mental clarity through a series of mental and physical practices that can help you overcome the typical triggers that lead to a lack of mental clarity in the first place. This includes mentally learning how to overcome emotions and stressors that may prevent mental clarity and physically creating a space around you that does not stimulate additional stress and mental clutter.

To begin mastering your mindset to reduce mental clutter, you need to start learning how to manage and overcome stress. The three ways that psychologists most recommend doing this is through developing a routine, learning how to tap into "flow," and preventing yourself from multitasking. Routines are particularly powerful when combined with the abstinence from multitasking because they help you get into a system where you know exactly what you need to do and when. This results in you staying focused and on-task longer because you know exactly what you need to be doing and you trust that there is enough time in your day for you to achieve everything, so you stop trying to do it all at once. At first, getting into a routine will be challenging as you are likely already used to being all over the place and living in mental chaos, but as you begin to foster a daily routine that does not require you to multitask, it will get easier. In regard to getting into your "flow" state, both having a routine and staying on track with one specific task at a time will help you get into the flow and find your groove in getting things done.

To begin mastering your physical environment for the sake of developing mental clarity, the task is quite simple: declutter. You need to maintain a clean and welcoming environment that does not have too much for your eye to focus on or look at, as this helps keep your mind clear as well. By keeping your environment clean and relaxing, you can ensure that you will not be overwhelmed by environmental distractions that may prevent you from getting focused or staying focused. This includes keeping your home clean and comforting while also favoring other environments that are more comfortable and relaxing as well, including when you go out for entertainment. Of course, enjoying upbeat and busy environments from time to time can be a great way to build excitement; spending too much time in these environments can further increase stress and decrease your mental clarity. Seek to spend more of your downtime in environments such as relaxing cafes, calm restaurants, quiet parks, and other comforting places. You should spend time in these places with friends when hanging out, but also on your own so that you can break away from the hustle and bustle of your daily life to get some calm and peace away from your normal routines. This really helps to detach your mind from everyday stress and keep you more in tune and in sync with your body and mind.

Learning to Remain Unbiased

Being biased means that you are approaching life with a very specific set of opinions and perceptions on the world around you and that you are attempting to fit everything in your life into these perceptions. Anytime something happens in your world, you will be quick to judge it and attempt to formulate an opinion on it, which can quickly result in you generating unnecessary suffering. Think about it: how often has something happened around you that should have been irrelevant to you but generated a significant amount of stress in your life for no apparent reason? Maybe your friend did something when you were nowhere near them, and it had no impact on you whatsoever, but you were upset with them because of the very fact that they would do such a thing. Or, maybe a coworker didn't get something done the day before, so you had to do it and you were angry about it because, even though it didn't change the fact that you still had to be at your job for 8 hours, now you had one more thing to do. Perhaps your judgment and anger get even more trivial sometimes, like when you are driving and you see one person cut another person off, and you become angry because of an ignorant driver on the road. Even though they had absolutely no impact on you, your judgment on their behavior resulted in you growing angry with them and produced unnecessary suffering on your behalf.

In our society, we are not taught about how we can detach from our opinions and perceptions and see the world through unbiased eyes which often results in us developing feelings of anger, jealousy, and resentment towards other people. The problem is, these feelings are completely unnecessary because, in many cases, the experiences that lead to these emotions do not even concern us, and if they do, the impact they have on us is minuscule.

Two things work against us that impact our tendency to be biased towards negativity in our lives: negativity bias and a society of individuals who are not consciously aware of their own negativity bias. Negativity bias is a survival mechanism that allows us to recall negative experiences that we have had so that we can avoid having them again. From a survival standpoint, negativity bias makes a lot of sense and can be highly useful in helping us avoid, say, getting eaten by a cougar in the middle of the forest. Unfortunately, it doesn't do us much good living in a society where we are mostly safe from the world around us. Instead, it often leads to us feeling intensely negative about things that do not really matter, and it can grow into full-blown pessimism if we are not taught to manage our negativity bias.

What happens when you have an entire community of people not managing their negativity bias is a community of people who are negative and pessimistic. This negativity spreads like wildfire and can cause several people to feel far more intense feelings of negativity and anger within just a few minutes. You have probably experienced it yourself: when you walk into your office and your boss is in a bad mood, and then suddenly the entire office building seems to be in a bad mood as well, including yourself. Negativity bias can produce serious negative consequences when people are not consciously aware of what it is and how it is negatively impacting their lives.

The best way to remain unbiased is to become self-aware and start paying attention to how your own negativity works and how you may be contributing to your own negative feelings. By recognizing your behaviors and the way that you contribute to negativity in your own life, you can start understanding how it impacts you and how your own perceptions are impacting your mood. As a result, you can start opening your mind to seeing your daily experiences from all angles and recognizing that nothing is ever as it seems, even if you have plenty to convince you otherwise. Try and see things from everyone's perspective and, as you do, detach from your own perspective enough to be unbiased from your experiences and perception.

As you do, suddenly that person that cut you off becomes a human in your mind, and you realize that they may just be someone who is rushing to the hospital to have their baby or home to see their family that they miss so dearly. Your boss who was previously arrogant and selfish may just be someone who came from a tough youth and had to fight their way to the top and has never let go of their fighting spirit. Your friend who made a poor decision when they were out on the weekend is just a human who decided for themselves, and one that had absolutely no impact on you whatsoever. And you, you become a human who cares deeply about everyone else, to the point that you have let their actions impact your own emotions. Everyone becomes a lot more *human* when you choose to release your bias and see people, and situations, for what they truly are.

Rationally Responding to Passionate Emotions

Emotions can be *intense,* and in a person who lacks mental toughness, they can be crippling. In the psychological field, when intense emotions overcome someone and cloud their rational judgment, it is known as "emotional hijacking." Emotional hijacking is most common in people who lack the ability to remain unbiased and see things rationally, so they end up experiencing intense, passionate emotions that are difficult to navigate through. This is where stoicism comes into play: it emphasizes the importance of handling these intense, passionate emotions through the power of mental resiliency and toughness.

Learning how to respond rationally to your emotional responses takes time as it requires you to learn first how to begin changing your instinctive response to emotional experiences. For example, when you experience sadness, it is likely that you have an instinctive habitual response to that sadness that begins occurring almost immediately after the sadness is triggered. Maybe you begin crying, even if it is just a small amount of sadness, or perhaps you find yourself getting angry because you were raised to believe that sadness was something to be ashamed about. This type of immediate response can trigger an even more intense emotional response, all of which launches as a habit of the initial emotion being triggered. For that reason, the first step in developing freedom from your intense and passionate emotional responses is to start by understanding what triggers are causing them. When you can begin to identify your emotional triggers, you can start to pinpoint the exact moment that your habitual emotional responses are preparing to launch and you can interrupt them with a more conscious response.

Say you are at work one day and your boss lost a piece of paperwork that you are *sure* you gave them, but they insist that it is your fault that the piece is missing. Perhaps this is a very important piece that places a lot of pressure on both you and your boss, and the fact that it is missing and you cannot prove that it was not you who lost it means that your job could be on the line. A stressful experience like this could easily trigger you to become angry and, if you were acting passionately, it could result in a massively angry outburst. This outburst would add to the stress of the situation and may result in you losing your job because of how unprofessionally you handled yourself during a challenging experience. As a result, you would experience even greater discomfort and anger, as well as a significantly higher amount of suffering due to your own emotional response.

If, however, you were to recognize that intense anger is starting to boil up and you were to choose to respond differently, you may start regaining rational control over yourself before your emotions boiled over. You might then find yourself being able to level out your emotions and support your boss in finding or replacing the important paperwork so that you could both calm down from the stress of the experience and move on. It may seem unreasonable for you to have to correct your bosses mistake. However, if you weigh the pros and cons of both sides of the situation, you may realize that this is a significantly smaller amount of suffering than if you were to react emotionally.

Building Mental Resiliency

Part of mental toughness is being able to bounce back from challenging situations time and again. Lindsay Teague Moreno, a self-made millionaire, claims that her mental resiliency is exactly what got her to her entrepreneurial success. In her words, she claimed that she could be at work all day and get knocked down over and over all day long and still show up the next day and walk in the door ready to work. Individuals who have experienced any capacity of personal or professional success in their lives will always tell you that their ability to get back up and try again was the exact reason for their success. Our society even has a series of quotes around this very topic that are intended to help people recognize the value of mental resiliency. Quotes like "get back on the horse," "fall seven times, get up eight," "no hoof, no horse," or "it's just a bad day, not a bad life" are all meant to remind us about the power of our mental resiliency. Still, not everyone is fully aware of how to tap into this resiliency and actually use it to change their lives.

In stoicism, building mental resiliency means that you can allow yourself to bounce back from intense emotions quicker, allowing you to regain ration in even the most challenging of situations. As you begin to develop your mental resiliency, you will find that enduring emotionally trying situations becomes easier because you are capable of bouncing back emotionally. In many experiences we have in life, a lack of mental resiliency can lead to an increase in emotions because, not only do you find yourself facing emotional struggles, but you also find yourself ill-equipped to overcome them. As a result, you may fear the feeling of being trapped in your emotions or unable to overcome them. This fear or uncertainty does not rise because you truly cannot overcome your emotions, but because you are not yet equipped with what you need to do so, which leaves you feeling fearful. Rationally, you cannot think of how you can reasonably get through your emotional struggles, so as your emotions grow, your irrational mind kicks in and leaves you feeling as though these emotions may never change. For this reason, mental resiliency will help you not only overcome life challenges but also emotional challenges and develop your stoicism more strongly.

Building the type of mental resiliency that is going to allow you to bounce back from challenging times takes patience and practice, but if you keep at it, you will discover that it's actually not as hard as it may seem. In fact, in most circumstances, it is simply about shifting your perspective and realizing that not everything is as challenging as it may seem. When you can begin considering your life through a particular perspective that actually serves your growth, rather than one that keeps you trapped in the belief that you can't make it happen, mental resiliency becomes easier. This is because you begin looking at things with the desire to grow through them and succeed, rather than feeling trapped in fear of the challenges that you face.

Creating this perspective takes practice as you begin conditioning yourself to look for ways forward, rather than admitting defeat and choosing to stay where you are at. This may sound simple enough, but for many people, the practice of changing their habitual thought patterns is particularly challenging, especially if you have never consciously taken control over your thoughts before. The best way to do this is to begin by having a mantra that you can carry with you to support you in staying clear on your goals so that you can regain mental control over your experience. Your mantra can be anything from "I choose not to react until I decide how to respond" to "I can overcome this." Once you choose a mantra, repeat it to yourself every time you face challenges in your life, particularly those around your emotions. This way, you can start conditioning yourself to endure trying times so that you no longer find yourself trapped in the false beliefs of being incapable of overcoming challenges.

After repeating your mantra to yourself, you need to begin consciously changing the way that you are viewing the situation so that you can take yourself out of victim mentality and start putting yourself into a victor mentality. A common tool for reframing challenging experiences is swapping out "Why is this happening to me?" to "How is this happening for me?" or "What can I learn from this?" When you begin to look at situations with the desire to either develop a greater understanding around them or to develop a solution, it becomes easier for you to bounce back. This is because your mind becomes focused on how you can move forward, rather than fearful and afraid of moving forward at all.

Maintaining Your Mental Toughness in Challenging Times

One place where many life changes tend to fall flat is when we are faced with particularly difficult challenges that trigger us in all of the most uncomfortable ways possible. If you have ever tried to make major changes in your life, chances are you have found yourself completely abandoning all of your adjustments as soon as things got really challenging because you were ill-equipped for what you needed to stay on track. I don't want you going through all of the efforts of building stoicism in your life only to find yourself experiencing major setbacks when you face challenges, so I have highlighted some great tools for you to stay on track even when it's a challenge.

Step 1: Slow Down

The first thing you need to do any time you face a challenge in your life that has you wanting to jump into old patterns and conditioning is to slow down. When you slow down, you give yourself the capacity to ease up on your emotional reaction and restore your ability to make a rational response to the situation at hand. Sometimes, when you are really in the heat of things, drawing back on your passion can be quite challenging, and you may find yourself struggling to stay aligned with your new stoic ways. In these situations, you may do best to completely remove yourself from the situation for a few minutes before returning with a clearer, more rational frame of mind. If you are pressed on time, a simple few minutes in the bathroom intentionally calming down and gaining some perspective over the situation can help you improve your response when you head back into the friction of a passionate situation.

If you have more time, consider slowing down your approach altogether and breaking it down into smaller steps. By paying attention to the next step, and then the next step, and then the next one, you prevent yourself from looking too far out into the future and give yourself time to make better choices *now*. You also give yourself the opportunity to see that the situation is not as large or scary as it may have seemed in the first place, which can draw back on some of the feelings of fear and frustration and allow you to address it with more rational thinking.

Step 2: Get Some Perspective

Once you have slowed the situation down, you need to get some perspective around it. Start by getting some perspective on how big the situation truly is so that you can remind yourself that virtually nothing is impossible to face, even if it seems gigantic and scary early on. Instead of allowing yourself to sit and be intimidated by the challenges that you face, sit and spend some time trying to understand them and trying to reframe them for yourself. Focus on how you can frame the challenge so that it seems manageable and achievable, rather than overwhelming and scary.

Then, go on to start searching for ways that you can overcome the challenge or even parts of the challenge as soon as possible. If you do not have all of the answers yet, start in the areas that you understand and move on from there. This way, you can at least get started and begin achieving success in overcoming your challenge. As you go along, you will likely learn everything you need to overcome your challenge even further, thus allowing you to move forward completely. Before you know it, your challenge will be a thing of the past and you will have successfully overcome it.

Step 3: Ask for Help

If you are really struggling with a challenge or if you do not have the answers you need to proceed, it is never wrong to ask for help in overcoming your challenge. Reaching out for someone who knows how to help you with your specific challenge is a great way to learn what you need to move forward successfully. Whether you need a counselor to help you manage your emotions, a coach to help you manage your time or your business strategies, or a friend to help you manage your thoughts, there is always someone out there who can help you. Simply be willing to reach out and know what it is that you need, and you can feel confident that someone will be on the other side to help you. Remember, asking for help is not a sign of weakness, but recognizing that we need help is a demonstration of strength.

Chapter 3: Discipline of Self

After you have built your foundation of mental toughness, you need to build your discipline of self. This discipline is going to help you continue building your mental toughness and conditioning yourself to use that mental toughness to develop your stoicism. As you develop your self-discipline, you will discover how you can start managing yourself through challenging emotional experiences, as well as how you can create a life that avoids unnecessary suffering. This is going to enable you to have the resiliency and knowledge to help you choose to respond to situations, rather than to react to challenging situations as they arise. Through this, you will be more stoic in your responses, which will lead to less suffering and greater growth in your life both personally and professionally.

In this chapter, we are going to focus on areas of self-discipline that are going to directly support you in managing your emotions better, as well as reducing the amount of unnecessary suffering you may face directly through your actions. This way, you can start living a life that does not produce unnecessary challenges and a life that has a greater self-discipline in facing the challenges that arise.

Accepting Yourself

Self-acceptance is one of the most powerful forms of self-discipline that you can embrace because it allows you to accept yourself as you are and stop putting pressure on yourself to be someone that you are not. Self-acceptance does not mean that you are not willing to look for opportunities to grow, but instead, that you are willing to accept when you are not embodying the growth that you wish to represent in each moment. When you accept yourself, forgiving yourself for mistakes and accepting that you are human and experience human experiences, including emotions, become significantly easier because you stop resenting yourself for your human nature. This means that any time you make a mistake, fail to move forward due to a lack of understanding, or experience an unwanted emotional outburst or setback, you accept yourself in spite of what happened. With true self-disciplined self-acceptance, you accept yourself even in the times when you feel that you have acted unacceptably because you accept yourself for exactly who you are in every single moment.

Being able to accept yourself this deeply can be challenging, especially in a society where we are often taught that we are only able to be accepted when we act or behave in a certain way. However, it is imperative as it allows you to accept yourself and love yourself even when you act 'wrongly,' which prevents the unnecessary pain and suffering associated with *not* accepting yourself. It also ensures that you are willing to move on quicker because you do not hold yourself back through your own contempt and hatred towards your unacceptable actions and behaviors. So, not only does it allow you to prevent the unnecessary suffering of a lack of self-acceptance, but it also allows you to prevent the unnecessary suffering of everything that follows that lack of self-acceptance.

Accepting yourself deeply and unconditionally takes time and practice, but it is essential if you want to experience true growth in your life. For that reason, you need to devote time every day to intentionally affirming your self-acceptance to yourself and your willingness to stay in acceptance with yourself even during challenging times. Of course, this is not always easy to achieve, so you are going to need to practice this every single day, even when it feels challenging or you feel as though you truly do not accept yourself at that moment. Realize that the thing you are not accepting of when you make a mistake in your life is not *you* personally, but your behavior and the consequences of that behavior. When you realize that you yourself are not the unacceptable one but your behavior was, it becomes easier to realize that you are still worthy of acceptance, even if your behavior was out of alignment.

Another great way to start building self-acceptance is to start journaling every time you feel that you are struggling to accept yourself. Writing down the reasons why you feel like you do not accept yourself and spending some time understanding your own true feelings and experiences can help you move beyond your unwillingness to accept yourself. This is because often when you see what you are thinking on paper, you realize how unkind or unrealistic it is, and it becomes easier for you to disown that way of thinking. You grow to realize how it is not serving you or how it is actually harming you, and you discover that there may be a better way: such as choosing self-acceptance.

Accepting Things Beyond Yourself

Acceptance with self-discipline needs to go beyond self-acceptance and into the acceptance of everything and experiences that you have in your life, too. When you live a life where you frequently do not accept what is happening around you or the people who you are surrounded by, it can present many unnecessary experiences of suffering. This suffering can arise because you feel intense emotions to everything around you on a consistent basis, for a myriad of different reasons. For example, perhaps, because you are unable to accept your family as they are, you find yourself angry and annoyed every time you are in their presence. As a result, you are unable to enjoy the presence of your family even if you genuinely feel as though you love them, which can lead to suffering. You may feel as though you are obligated to see them due to your love for them and your familial connection, or because you will experience alternative forms of suffering if you do not. So, whether you choose to see your family and suffer in their presence or avoid your family and suffer in their absence, you will still experience suffering because of your own inability to accept your family.

The same can be said for your job, your financial well-being, your home, your community, and anything else that exists beyond yourself. When you cannot accept the things around you, your surroundings become a constant source of discomfort and pain which can lead to you having constant feelings of depression, disappointment, frustration, and anguish. Learn to accept situations and people as they enable you to bypass unnecessary suffering and begin cultivating a deeper sense of appreciation for the life that you have. As a result, you cannot only avoid suffering but also cultivate contentment through the very act of acceptance.

Learning how to accept the things beyond you starts with you discovering how you can tolerate the presence of various things, experiences, or people without taking everything so personally. When you realize that other people's actions or behaviors are not an attack on you personally, as well as with your circumstances and things in your environment, acceptance becomes easier. This is because you can realize that the world around you is not victimizing you, but instead, you are simply experiencing it. It is within your mind that the victimizing begins when you genuinely believe that every person, thing, and experience is intended to be a personal attack on you.

You can also develop a greater sense of acceptance by recognizing that, in many cases, your perception of other people has something to teach you about yourself. By seeking out what that lesson may be, you offer yourself the capacity to understand why you are so bothered by others and how you can stop choosing to not accept others based on who they are, or circumstances based on what they are. See why you are so deeply bothered and why it feels as though you cannot overlook these things, and choose to find ways to overlook them and move on anyway. You always have a choice in your life, and you can choose to either let go of great friendships over small things or to accept things as they are and find a way to tolerate the fact that you cannot control others around you.

Maintaining Virtue and Kindness

Stoicism is not just about tolerating those around you and ignoring your own emotions, but rather, it is about learning how to manage those emotions and find more kind-hearted ways through them. For example, if you experience anger towards a certain situation, choosing to express that anger through words and finding a resolution calmly would become your goal. This way, you can experience your anger, discover a solution, and move forward from your anger without engaging in behaviors that can cause major consequences for both yourself and those around you. In stoicism, this is the ultimate goal because, through proper and intentional management of your emotions, you can avoid engaging in major blowouts that can lead to further emotional struggles such as guilt and shame.

In life, your virtue refers to your behaviors and how they reflect your moral standards in life. If you are someone with great virtue, then you are someone who has high morals and who lives up to those morals through your behaviors and your actions. Historically, virtue also reflected ones' purity physically and mentally, so it often involved maintaining your virginity until marriage so that you would be completely pure. In modern days, a virtue often coincides with kindness because people who possess high morals believe that those around them deserve to be treated with kindness and respect, so being kind to others is a symbol of virtue in a person.

Maintaining your own virtue and kindness truly is self-discipline because we are often compelled to behave in ways that abandon virtue and kindness based on the experience of our emotions. When you experience frustration, for example, you may become snappy and harsh in your tone, making everyone around you feel as though you are not respecting them and their feelings. Chances are, this reaction is not intentional or even conscious; it is a habitual emotional response to having your feelings triggered in a particular way. Likely, it stems from not having a strong education around how to handle your emotions properly.

When you want to develop and maintain your virtue, your goal is to begin identifying what morals you desire to live by and seeking the opportunity to live by those morals in your life every single day. Common morals include or relate to humility, kindness, abstinence, chastity, patience, liberality, and diligence, which are the opposites of the seven deadly sins that are commonly taught in many religions. These virtues ultimately seek to shape people into being individuals who are willing to show up and serve not only themselves but their communities by supporting everyone around them in living in a positive life. When you consider these virtues, consider what they mean to you and how they impact your life, and then declare that you are prepared to begin living by these virtues every single day. Then, every single day, do what you can to live in alignment with these virtues and be willing to accept yourself when you do not. As you continue practicing and reminding yourself of these virtues, you will find that it becomes much easier for you to grow as a person and to maintain your virtue and kindness along the way.

Making Peace with Your Past

Many people abandon self-discipline due to guilt, shame, and residual fear that they hold onto from their past experiences. It is not uncommon to live a life where you are shaped by your past, particularly as humans who have the capacity to remember it and to remember the emotions that coincided with these memories. One of the vices of evolution is that, in being able to remember our past so that we can improve our chances of survival, we can also remember our past to the point that it retriggers trauma within us on an ongoing basis. Making peace with your past by healing unresolved traumas and challenges and accepting what you cannot change is a powerful way to release yourself from the grips of your own history and permit yourself to move forward.

When you choose to move forward without letting your past hold you back, it becomes easier for you to accept yourself more wholly and completely, including who you were in the past and who you desire to be in the future. You stop denying yourself the right to a joyful and evolutionary future because you no longer punish yourself for your experiences in the past. So, it becomes easier for you to possess even greater levels of virtue, kindness, acceptance, and mental toughness. Thus, making peace with your past directly supports your ability to develop your stoicism and become a more ethical person as a whole.

Making peace with your past takes a significant amount of emotional healing, and may not always be ideal to do on your own. Healing from your past is going to require you to personally go within and discover what needs to be healed and do some of the work yourself, while also reaching out for help whenever help is needed. By reaching out for help, you ensure that you have the support and acceptance needed to help you overcome challenging experiences in your life and grow as a person. However, the reality of inner healing is that no one else can do it for you, so you are going to need to be willing to endure the emotional aspects of healing on your own. As you do, you will find that accepting your past becomes easier because you come to peace with everything that has happened to you and how you have been impacted by various people and experiences in your life. This type of healing brings closure to painful experiences, which is often all that is needed for us to make peace with our pasts.

Overcoming Procrastination and Distractions

One of the biggest ways that people generate pain in their own lives, aside from being unwilling to accept the things beyond their control, is procrastination. Procrastination can be caused by many things, and no matter what the root cause is, it virtually always causes severe setbacks and troubles for the people who do not teach themselves to overcome this unhelpful behavior. From causing a significant amount of unnecessary stress for having to catch up last minute to causing guilt and shame for things not being completed on time, many negative setbacks can be derived from procrastination.

Overcoming procrastination in your own life requires you to start by getting to the root cause of your procrastination and finding ways to bypass that root cause so that you can get past it. In many cases, the root cause is emotional. With procrastination, you may be procrastinating something because it brings you pain, or because the alternative brings you joy. For example, you may procrastinate healing from your past because revisiting parts of your past is a painful experience for you, so you are afraid to get into it. Alternatively, you may procrastinate getting a task done for work because watching TV brings greater joy than crunching numbers or putting together presentations.

By discovering what it is that you are being motivated by more (the avoidance of pain or the desire for comfort), you can begin finding ways to work through the work that needs to be done. Some ideas include going through the process slowly so that it is not too overwhelming, breaking it down into manageable steps, or rewarding yourself for achieving success along the way. These types of small adjustments to your approach can make it easier for you to stop avoiding the process so that you can get it done and get on with your life. Once you have determined what adjustments you want to make, the last thing you have to do is get up and actually get started. For some people, this will be plenty to help them get up and get past their behavior of procrastination.

For others, these may not be enough to keep them on track, and they may find themselves backsliding into procrastination rather quickly. If you are this type of person, you need to find a way to implement some strategies to help you avoid procrastination even after you have already started. One great strategy is to find out what is distracting you or tempting you to procrastinate and avoiding that distraction as much as you possibly can. Another way is to implement a distraction time limit for yourself, as this may be more affected for people who truly cannot overcome distractions in their lives. If you are someone who gets distracted and genuinely struggle to get focused again after even a minor distraction, first off, realize that you are actually extremely normal. Recent studies have suggested that the average attention span of a human is 2.5 seconds before they become distracted once again and need to regain focus. By the way, that means that our attention span is now shorter than that of a goldfish if you were wondering!

By giving yourself a distraction break every now and again, which is simply one to three minutes to engage in a distraction and get it out of your system, you relieve your mind off the urge to get distracted and help yourself regain focus. If you find that you are getting distracted *a lot*, consider starting with frequent one-minute distraction breaks and then spacing them out further and further so that you can train yourself to increase your attention span. This way, you can condition yourself to avoid distractions without expecting yourself to be able to change your behaviors overnight completely.

Moving in Alignment with Your Goals

Another method of self-discipline that is seldom taught, but highly necessary in reducing the amount of suffering that you experience in your life, is learning how to move in alignment with your goals. Our modern society has been largely built on following a "cookie cutter" lifestyle for a long time, which means that many people are doing what they *should* be doing and are experiencing no joy or satisfaction out of it. People are pursuing jobs that they should be pursuing, getting married and having kids because they should be, engaging in hobbies because they should be, and ultimately building entire lives around the word "should." These days, there is a popular saying that goes: "Don't should all over yourself" and I think it is highly applicable here.

Doing everything in your life because you believe that is what you should be doing and because you are afraid of doing things differently only leads to you being unhappy and depressed in the long run. This is because, as humans, our emotional side needs to be nourished and taken care of and you simply cannot do that if you are constantly doing what you "should" be doing. Instead, you will find that you are building an entire life that you don't particularly care for and, because of that lack of caring, you struggle to generate motivation to actually make it happen. This all spirals into deep levels of disappointment and frustration which can ultimately lead to you living an unfulfilling life and suffering far more than you need to be.

If you want to experience true freedom and joy in your life, as well as the inner strength required to minimize your suffering, you need to start moving in alignment with your personal goals. Not only will this help you feel more fulfilled, but it will also bring a renewed sense of positivity into your life which will make acting in alignment with stoicism far easier. When you are generally a happy person, dealing with your challenging and passionate emotions becomes easier because they are not piling up and causing you to feel an intense need to release them.

You can move in alignment with your goals by determining two primary goals for yourself: who you want to be in life and what you want to have in life. By determining what these goals are, you can start setting personal rules for yourself to help you move in alignment with these goals. For example, if your goal is to be a stoic person, you will want to set rules for yourself that you will only behave in ways that cultivate your stoicism and that support you in experiencing less overall suffering in your life. If your goal is to have more money and a better house, then you would begin behaving in ways that allow you to save more money and work towards acquiring your better home.

When you set goals for yourself and you begin moving towards them, every time you see yourself making successful progress in your life, you start to feel more empowered and motivated to keep going. This can add an enriching and fulfilling feeling into your life that supports you in being happier overall. Through this, your life becomes less about suffering and more about creating one that makes you happy to wake up and enjoy your day to day experience. Many benefits can come from following personal goals, both in terms of materialistic goals and goals for yourself and your personal growth.

Chapter 4: Discipline of Action

Now that you have the inner strength and personal power required to begin moving your internal processes in alignment with stoicism, it is time for you to start bringing stoicism into your discipline of action! Your action is where you begin to allow your inner thoughts and processes develop so that you can start actually behaving stoically. This is where stoicism really comes into play because your stoic actions and behaviors will begin changing your life as you enforce them and embody them going forward. Through disciplined actions, you are going to start behaving in a way that shows emotional constraint, allowing you to use your emotions effectively, and that is ethical towards yourself and those around you.

In this chapter, we are going to discover what disciplined actions are, how they align with stoicism, and what specific actions you need to begin disciplining to embody a stoic lifestyle. Remember, stoicism heavily relies on ethical behaviors that align with virtue and morality, so your goal here is to begin acting in an ethical way that aligns with high morals. Through this behavior, you are not only going to increase your ability to embody stoicism, but you are also going to quite literally change the way that you engage with the world around you beyond your own inner thoughts and experiences.

Remember, changing behaviors like this can be quite a daunting task because you are going to be changing nearly everything about yourself likely. Since most modern humans are still highly driven by emotions, teaching yourself to become more driven by rational thought and reason without losing the value of your emotions can take time. You are truly going to be conditioning yourself into becoming a new person, which takes consistent time and practice. Furthermore, you may find that now your stoic behaviors are moving into your physical actions, the people around you start treating you differently. Those who are not benefiting from your changes may attempt to push you back into your old habits, and those who appreciate your new adjustments may start gravitating towards you in a higher degree. This means that your circle of friends and acquaintances may change as you, too, change in a rather drastic manner. That being said, deep acceptance of yourself and those around you as well as an unwillingness to revert to old behaviors will be essential in helping you completely embrace the discipline of action.

Controlling Your Emotional Passion and Expression

Where true stoicism comes into play, and not the exploitation of it that was encouraged by those who profited off of emotional repression, is when you learn how to actually control your emotional passion and expression. Through controlling your emotional passion and expression, you teach yourself to harness your emotional power and turn it into a productive tool to help you advance further in your life. For example, anger around activism that is not turned into blind rage can instead be used to passionately change people's opinions and support the true cause of the activist. Passion about the need for more love in your relationship can be harnessed to produce changes in your relationship, rather than to produce jealousy and anger around the fact that changes are not being made. When you learn how to control your emotional passion and expression, you allow yourself to use that passion alongside rational thinking to fuel the actions required to make changes in your life or the lives of those around you.

Learning how to control your emotional passion is not only a form of emotional intelligence, but it is also a form of ethical behavior. By that I mean, stoicism believes that we should always act ethically no matter what we are doing, whether it is professional or personal. How you treat people, for example, should be ethical or of high moral standards so that you always treat people with the utmost respect and kindness in all circumstances. Behaving in this way ensures that you are always doing right by yourself and by those around you, which in turn earns you greater respect and appreciation from others.

If controlling your emotions and harnessing their power to stimulate change were easy, we would all be doing it. So it goes without saying that the balancing act of being able to experience emotional passion without expressing it intensely is challenging. Learning how to regain control over yourself amidst intense emotions requires you to slow down the experience and intentionally work with your emotions in a controlled manner. You can do this by noticing the moment an emotion begins to grow in intensity and review what the goal of that particular emotion is. For example: if you are jealous in your relationship, your goal is to develop security; if you are angry with how someone is treating you, your goal is to be treated better; and if you are grieving about a loss that you have endured, then your goal is to heal the pain.

Recognizing what your goal is with any particular emotion allows you to avoid becoming the victim of that emotion, and instead, become a person who can reasonably work his/her way through the emotion. It also prevents you from turning that emotion into a larger point of trauma or emotional suffering and enables you instead to use it to reduce your suffering overall. The next step is to begin acting in a way that works in alignment with your emotion's goal rather than your emotion itself. This is where the intense act of self-discipline comes into play: in holding yourself back from emotionally reacting and following through with your goal-based actions instead. In this situation, slowing down your approach to your resolution as much as possible will allow you to regularly check in with your goal and ensure that you are acting in alignment with it. If at any time you move out of alignment with your goal, then you will be checking in often enough to regain control over your emotions and adjust your approach.

Practicing emotional control and expression frequently enough will really be the key to developing deep control over your emotional expression. They say that you need to practice something at least 1,000 times before you completely master it, so trust that every time you have the opportunity to practice the emotional control you are working towards greater success. The more intentional you become and the more serious effort you put into regaining control over your emotions, the greater control you will have in the long run.

Acting in an Ethical Manner

In the early days of stoicism, a series of ethical actions were outlined that were intended to give stoics a set of rules to live by, so to speak. These rules were fairly simple and were intended to guide people through the proper resolutions of challenging experiences that they would face throughout their lives. The Stoics called these rules "appropriate acts" or "proper functions" and they were defined by behaving in a way that adhered to what reason persuaded them to do. So, rather than being persuaded by their emotions, the Stoics aimed to be persuaded by their rational thinking mind, or reason. Stoicism aims to achieve the process of justified, rational thinking so that every action is enacted in a way that honors both parties involved and works towards achieving a higher goal, rather than an immediate emotional goal.

For things that were not inherently good *or* bad, such as health, stoics aimed to maintain their health positively which allowed them to turn the act of maintaining good health into an ethical act. This way, they could walk in one with their human nature and harmonize their lifestyles through the act of maintaining good health. Another example was through the act of sacrificing ones' property, which could either be good or bad, depending on the circumstances at hand. If the act was done because it made a good, reasonable sense to do so, then it likely aligned with stoic's virtues and morals for ethical living. If it didn't adhere to reasonable persuasion, however, then sacrificing one's property was not an act of ethical morals and therefore was considered to be "bad". For example, someone was threatening the livelihood of your family if you did not sacrifice your property. In this case, it would make rational sense to sacrifice your property to protect the lives of your family, so sacrificing your property would be virtuous and ethical. If, however, the sacrifice was being made for personal fortune and well-being but would cost your family in some large way, then sacrificing your property would not be ethical and would be out of alignment with the stoic way of living.

If you want to act in an ethical manner true to stoic nature, you need to learn how to justify things based on rational and reasonable thinking and then act accordingly. In doing so, you bring your decision-making process into the heart of reason and out of the grips of emotions which can often lead to us doing things that are completely out of alignment with the greater good. If you want to act in true stoic nature, simply ask yourself: "Is this a reasonable decision to make? Can I reasonably justify this? Will it lead me towards my true goal, or away from it?" If the answers to these questions support your decision, chances are it is a true, ethical decision that is going to support your success. If the answer is no, then chances are you are acting out of alignment with ethics, and you need to reassess your proceedings to ensure that you are acting ethically towards yourself and everyone else involved in the situation with you.

Solving Your Problems Effectively

Learning how to act ethically and with control over your emotional passion and expression will not only help you refrain from producing unwanted consequences through your actions, but it will also help you when it comes to problem-solving. People who can bypass emotional intensity and tune into their rational thinking mind are often able to get a clearer understanding of their problems and choosing actions that will support them in discovering a genuine resolve. As you continue learning how to gain more control over your emotions and how you act on them, you should also begin diving into this major benefit of being able to tune into your rational thinking mind with greater clarity and intention.

Exercising your mind for problem-solving abilities is much easier once you have gained control over your emotions and have started tapping into your reasonable thinking mind. From there, all you need to do is begin developing the habit of looking at a problem from a bird's-eye view so that you can clearly see the entirety of the problem itself. If you are experiencing a problem that involves other people, seek to understand the problem from everyone's angle and get a clear understanding of what all your goals are so that you can work towards finding a solution that serves each of your goals. If you are experiencing a problem on your own, seek to understand the obstacles that are standing in your way and put them into perspective. See them for what they truly are, avoid making them appear larger to yourself, and get clear on what it will actually take for you to reasonably overcome these obstacles in an ethical way. That way, you can start producing action steps for you to take that will help you move towards your goal without compromising your moral standards.

After you have mentally produced a solution to overcoming your goals, the next step is to actually act that solution out. Again, you are going to need to put in a lot of work towards overcoming your personal challenges such as your emotional habits that are going to encourage you to behave in the way that you have always behaved. You will need to consistently practice and remain intentional towards changing your behavior so that, over time, it grows easier for you to behave in a more constrained and intentional manner.

Once you are able to combine your reasonable thinking and controlled emotional expression into your problem-solving abilities, you will have an incredibly powerful tool in your hands. This tends to be the most challenging time to combine emotional restraint with reasonable actions as problems can bring with them feelings of fear and desperation, in addition to the other emotions that arise. Learning how to navigate through these challenging times will put your stoicism to the ultimate test, and when you navigate these effectively, you can feel confident that your stoic development is working.

Acting with Discipline in Relationships

In relationships, it can be particularly challenging to act stoically because your emotions can be so much more intense. Love is an emotion that we all crave and need, and that can bring us great suffering and pain if we do not learn how to navigate alongside the emotion of love effectively. For many, love can be one of the most overwhelming emotions to experience because it tends to sweep through your entire body and hijack your mind with no warning signs. Then, from that state of emotional hijacking, other emotions have the capacity to squeeze into your emotional hijacking and take over how you express yourself. As a result, you can find yourself being completely backward in acting stoic in relationships, even if you are managing your stoicism well in other areas of your life.

These feelings are not exclusive to your romantic relationships, either, but instead in any relationship where love or deep admiration towards another human is present. When you experience love in your life, you need to be extra cautious and considerate towards your emotions and how you may be expressing your emotions in relation to love. For example, if you are continuing a relationship because you love the other person, but it brings you both tremendous suffering, then continuing the relationship or at least continuing it in a current way may not be ideal. You may need to adjust how you are approaching the relationship or consider terminating it altogether to eliminate the unnecessary suffering of both yourself and the other person.

Acting ethically in relationships truly requires you to deeply consider how both you and the other person are being impacted and whether or not the relationship makes reasonable sense as it is. If your relationship makes sense but the actions taking place within the relationship do not, then it may be time to reconsider how you treat each other and the respect that you have for each other. If your relationship no longer makes sense, or there is no way to restore it to a state where it can stop causing hurt, then it may be time to take a break from it or terminate the relationship altogether.

Always make sure that the way you treat your loved ones is respectful of both yourself and them, and that you never allow your emotions to persuade you to behave unreasonably. Be cautious to never let love get in the way of reason by frequently checking in with your behaviors and making sure that it makes reasonable sense to move forward in the way that you are. This way, you can always treat your loved ones, including yourself, with the respect and compassion that they deserve, whether that is experienced up close or from afar.

Moving Towards Professional Goals Ethically

Another area of your life where you need to begin developing self-discipline is in your professional life. Emotions tend to hold people back when they start behaving in an emotionally-driven manner at work, whether that is conscious or unconsciously driven. For example, being upset with your boss is one thing, but taking it out on your boss through a passionate expression of emotion can result in you being seen as unprofessional and unstable. It may even result in you losing your job due to an inability to function professionally while in the workplace. It is imperative that you learn how to manage your emotions properly so that you can behave in a controlled manner during professional experiences, ensuring to yourself and everyone around you that you are stable enough to handle professional duties.

Stoicism also needs to be reflected in your relationships with people in your professional life, no matter who they may be or what role they may play in your profession. From your boss to your coworkers or even your customers, you should always be handling yourself in a professional manner that honors your high ethics and moral standards. It may seem fun and harmless to engage in inappropriate relationships, behaviors or conversations with people relating to your career, but in the long run, it may not be the best idea. You never know how these types of seemingly harmless interactions could later impact the well-being of your career and lead to you experiencing troubles in moving forward. For example, your chummy relationship with your boss may make your present work life more enjoyable, but if it is not controlled through rational thinking, it may lead to them liking you but seeing someone else as a better fit for promotion. In this case, your overly friendly relationship may not be bad enough to get you fired, but it may cost you the professional respect and consideration of your boss.

You should always consider the reasonable reality of your professional career and how your behaviors and actions are moving you towards success. If it does not make reasonable sense to behave in the way that you are behaving, even if it seems harmless on the surface, you need to begin adjusting your behaviors. This way, you are seen as professional and competent, and it is *you* who will excel faster than anyone else due to your reasonable behaviors.

Chapter 5: Achieving the Goal of Stoicism

You are officially equipped with all of the basic understanding that you need to embody to begin achieving the goal of stoicism. Hopefully, you have already begun practicing and embodying some of the teachings from earlier in this audiobook, but if you haven't yet, do not worry: we are going to begin applying these practices right now. In this chapter, you are going to learn about what it takes for you to actually achieve the goal of stoicism and practices you can start using right away. These tools are all powerful in incorporating into your lifestyle to help you achieve the goal of stoicism one step at a time.

Making total life changes can be trying and it takes a particular degree of devotion to officially embody the goals of total lifestyle changes, including the goal of stoicism. Be sure to proceed through this chapter while applying each step at your own pace and searching for ways to incorporate it into your personal way of living. Everyone will have a slightly different take on how they personally can develop and embody lifestyle changes, so do not be afraid to make your own personalizations to these tools. As long as the heart of the tools remains the same, your application can be done in any way needed to achieve *your* goal of stoicism.

Understanding the Goal of Modern Stoicism

Let's begin by refreshing your mind on what the goal of modern stoicism truly is. You already know that the goal of stoicism, in general, is to reduce suffering by embodying an ethical way of living, but you may wonder exactly what that means or what that looks like in a modern world. After all, the world we are living in today is significantly different from the world that existed in ancient Greek and Roman times. So, let's take a deep look into what modern stoicism looks like and the goals that it aspires to accomplish.

Despite advancing a great deal in society, many humans continue to live lives that are highly steeped in stress and suffering. It has almost become a part of the societal norm to make a joke out of living the "typical modern lifestyle", which regularly involves working at a job you dislike with a boss you don't respect and doing things out of obligation instead of personal desire. Unfortunately, just because you can make light of your suffering does not mean it does not exist any longer. If you truly want to live the stoic way, you need to start taking action towards actually reducing or eliminating unnecessary suffering in your life so that you can begin living a life of greater emotional freedom.

In modern life, this looks like finding a way to accept your life as it is right now and setting goals to improve your life so that you can start experiencing greater joy and freedom. Perhaps for you, this looks like accepting your present career and the fact that you cannot get what you want from it and setting the goal to pursue a career that you are more passionate about. Or, maybe it is learning how to accept your family as they are and learning to set new boundaries so that their behaviors no longer personally affect you, allowing you to enjoy their company more without being hurt by them so much. It may even require you to terminate some friendships and relationships and begin setting higher standards on how you are willing to let others treat you and how you are going to treat others so that you can proceed with a better life overall.

Stoicism is an opportunity to stop letting emotions drive you into suffering so that you can begin moving forward rationally. Through reasonable thinking and problem-solving, you can stop letting your emotions lead you into believing that you are trapped and start letting your sense of reason remove you from the rut that you are currently stuck in. This will likely look like a total life transformation, particularly if you are presently living a life of intense suffering and struggle. Although the endurance of this transformation may be challenging, particularly as you lose those comforts and habits that have led to your suffering so far, the outcome will be more than worth it.

Advice from Stoics

These days, stoicism is broken down into two parts: modern stoicism and ancient stoicism. Modern stoicism is still highly driven by the teachings of ancient stoicism and the advice that these early philosophers shared with those who desired to embody and embrace the stoic way of living. While there is plenty of modern advice around stoicism making waves around the Internet, I want to provide you with some powerful and profound advice from ancient stoicism which is where it all began. Of course, this advice is going to be adjusted for the purposes of modern living, but I genuinely believe that connecting with the ancient roots of stoicism will help you embody it more accurately.

Below are five pieces of advice from ancient stoics that have been modernized so that you can use them in your modern life.

1. Change Only What You Can

Humans endure a great deal of suffering by generating a false sense of control over that which they cannot truly control. The belief that we can control other peoples' actions or decisions leads to us feeling a sense of suffering when our attempts at control betray us, and we do not actually gain the control we seek. As a result, we find ourselves struggling to accept the outcomes because we believe that there is either something fundamentally wrong with ourselves or something fundamentally wrong with those around us. The reality is that nothing is fundamentally wrong here, aside from the belief that you can in any way control anything beyond yourself.

Allow yourself to stop deluding yourself into believing that you can control anything or anyone other than yourself and start focusing on how you can control yourself. Pay attention to your personal responses and reactions to the world around you and start seeking opportunities to control those responses more effectively. The more you focus on changing yourself, including your perceptions, your thoughts, and your behaviors, the less unnecessary suffering you will experience through your own behaviors and beliefs.

2. Start Living Today

Procrastinating when it comes to creating a life that will be more fulfilling and enjoyable is one of the biggest acts of disservice that you could possibly do for yourself. Not only does it put off your ability to acquire what you desire, but it also results in you living in unnecessary suffering even longer as you attempt to uphold a lifestyle that does not genuinely light you up. Instead of putting it off, start focusing on living a better life today by choosing to accept yourself as you are and your past for what it is.

Look for opportunities to begin showing up passionately and ethically, find ways to build a life that is filled with meaning and purpose, and pursue your meaning and purpose rationally. Practice bringing your emotion into harmony with your reason and carrying yourself in a way that is respectful and kind to both yourself and those around you, and let yourself grow from there. Each day that you invest into living a better life, you add another day into it that you get to live free from unnecessary suffering and pain.

3. **Know That You Cannot Be Broken**

We have a tendency to place a lot of power into the hands of other people by believing that they can genuinely impact us through their actions. While the actions of others may impact our physical bodies and external circumstances, our souls can never be broken. The inner part of who you are will always remain intact and whole, and you can always choose to live in a way that honors this part of you. If you find yourself being abused or taken advantage of by others in your life, choose to remember that you cannot be broken and act as though you are whole and complete in spite of their behaviors. Not only will this minimize the pain that you endure, but it will also help you remain in control over your emotions and emotional expressions.

4. **"Don't burn the candle on both ends."**

There is an old saying that goes "Don't burn the candle on both ends" which essentially means that you should never try and endure more than you can reasonably handle. Without fully relaxing your mind and body and offering them the breaks that they need, you will be attempting to overdo it, and you will likely run yourself into a state of burnout. If you want to enjoy a happier and healthier life, you need to be able to maintain your physical and mental health and truly commit to the maintenance of it.

The emotional desire may be to do the things that make you feel comfortable, but the ethical and reasonable solution is to do the things that may not be as comforting now so that you can minimize your suffering later. By fiercely protecting your mental and physical health, you can maintain it for as long as possible.

5. Focus Inward on Yourself

Stoics believe that suffering comes from within, from our own perceptions and judgments of the world around us, and that this can lead to severe pain in our lives. For this reason, stoic advice is that anytime you experience the desire to judge someone else, you look within yourself to understand what that judgment means and where it is coming from.

If you are judging someone for their ill health, for example, look within and ask yourself why someone else's health would possibly impact you to the point of having your own personal suffering. Realize that you are not that intimately connected to anyone in your life, no matter how close your relationship with them may be, and that you are not required to suffer for the sake of others. Ask yourself why you are so attached to that form of suffering, and begin doing the inner healing and growth required to detach from suffering that is in no way relating to your personal experiences.

Daily Mindfulness Practices

A great way to achieve stoicism in your life is to begin practicing daily mindfulness practices. Practicing mindfulness is an excellent way to cultivate your self-awareness and to begin to recognize areas of your life where you may be increasing your level of suffering for no apparent reason. It also allows you to begin identifying where your emotions come into play and how they are impacting your daily living. When you take the time to understand your emotions and how they are affecting you, as well as your actions and how they are affecting you, you can audit your life as a whole and seek out opportunities for growth.

In Chapter 6, we will discuss many areas where you can cultivate your daily mindfulness practice, but in essence, you are going to want to start as soon as possible by developing your self-awareness. Start asking yourself "How am I doing?" or "How am I feeling?" and begin honestly answering these questions to yourself. This way, you can easily begin to identify how you are honestly doing in life and what may be contributing to those feelings that you are having. In instances where you recognize unnecessary suffering, you can begin understanding why that suffering exists and how you are contributing to it so that you can start untangling the suffering. Then, you can begin approaching similar experiences in the future more intentionally and mindfully so as to reduce the amount of suffering you experience.

To paint a picture of mindfulness in your mind, and how this powerful tool can help you overcome suffering, let's take a look at an average daily experience that many people can probably relate to in one way or another. Imagine you were to wake up one morning and you walked into the kitchen to pour yourself a cup of coffee, only to find that there was no coffee left in the house because you forgot to purchase some when you went to the store. In this moment, you may feel a surge of frustration leap through you as you realize that your favorite morning routine has been interrupted by your own forgetfulness. When your spouse awakens and comes into the kitchen, perhaps you start taking your frustration out on him/her because you are feeling upset about the coffee situation. In this situation, you are not expressing mindfulness nor tuning into your rational thinking mind to recognize that you are simply upset that your routine has been interrupted, and not towards your spouse in any way. However, if you are not thinking mindfully and acting stoically, you might instead simply take your emotions out on your partner and increase the level of unnecessary suffering that both of you endure that morning. As you can see, bringing mindfulness into your daily practice allows you to keep everything in perspective, stay self-aware around your own experiences and emotions, and have the consciousness to choose differently. Rather than choosing to act on your emotions, you can consciously choose to act on your reason instead and be kind to your partner despite your own inner frustrations.

A Morning Meditation for Stoicism

A great way to start your day out and develop your stoicism is to begin your day with a morning meditation designed specifically to help you achieve the very goal of stoicism. Meditations are great exercises because they allow you to gain a deeper sense of emotional control over yourself, while also giving you time to visualize what you desire for yourself and making it easier for you to manifest that into your reality. For a stoic meditation, you will want to use both the releasing of unwanted emotions and the development of a vision to help you increase your stoic behaviors and cultivate a deeper sense of emotional self-control.

You can start your morning meditation by simply relaxing into a basic breathing meditation at first. To do this, relax into a comfortable seated position on the floor or on a meditation cushion and start bringing your awareness to your breath. As you become aware of your breath, start gently guiding your breath to become more rhythmic by breathing in to the count of eight and breathing out to the count of eight, too. Doing this will bring your body into a state of comfortable relaxation that will help you ease into your meditative state. When you begin to feel more relaxed, allow yourself to enjoy a few minutes of basic meditation where you can simply relax and enjoy the experience. During this first part of your meditation, you are going to develop your ability to ground your emotions and build your mindfulness, thus increasing the mental toughness that you can carry with you throughout the day. This is going to help you in tuning into your rational thinking more consistently as well, which will keep you in alignment with your goal of stoicism.

After you have spent some time relaxing in a state of meditation, you want to begin moving into the state of visualization. Here, you want to visualize what your day would look like if you were behaving stoically and how that stoicism might change the way your day would look. Envision yourself approaching your day with a greater sense of reason and ration, and with the desire to develop a stronger ability to control your emotions. Consider certain parts of your day that are typically emotionally charged and consider what they might look like if you were to take greater control over those situations in your life. When you can begin to visualize alternative habits or responses to the things that you encounter in your life, behaving in a new way becomes easier because you are essentially planning what your different responses would be. Furthermore, you envisioning yourself behaving in a completely new way actually builds your confidence in your ability to behave differently too, because you have already "seen" yourself doing it. Your ability to imagine your better responses and your better life actually creates the skills that you need to begin developing better responses and a better life.

Philosophical Diaries

Stoicism is largely based on philosophy and belief of life having a certain purpose and meaning, particularly relating to behaving in a certain way both towards yourself and towards others in your life. Stoicism itself already has a list of ethics and virtues that outlines what it is, but that does not mean that you cannot use a diary to begin developing your own belief around what stoicism is to you and what it means to you personally. When you begin to develop your own beliefs around what stoicism is and how it works, you can start really embodying and embracing this way of life in a personal manner. This allows you to make it yours and develop a personal passion, purpose, and reason for following this way of life and embodying it in your own everyday experiences.

Keeping a philosophical diary does not only support you in making stoicism more personal to yourself and your own interpretation, but it also supports you in discovering more about yourself. Through these journals, you can start digging into what life means to you, what you believe the purpose of life is, what morals and virtues you personally hold value for, and what you desire more of in life. These types of exploration topics will help you really develop an understanding around yourself and why you may behave the way you do and experience the emotions that you experience. For example, if you believe that a high moral standard is to respect your family and accept them deeply no matter who they are, then it may make sense as to why you grow so frustrated when they do something that you perceive to be unacceptable. Or, it may make sense as to why you struggle to relate with people who do not also hold their families to such great value in their own lives.

The more you understand yourself in this intimate way, the easier it is for you to develop your mindfulness even further and create reasons behind why you behave, think, and feel the way you do from experience to experience. As you explore yourself even further, identifying your own feelings and experiences from moment to moment becomes easier, and you can start carrying yourself more intentionally. Not only are you able to identify your actual habits and behaviors, but you are also able to identify how you can align them to work towards your overall goals because you now know what those goals actually are. As a result, you can experience greater growth in your life.

Studying the Art of Stoicism

When you make a total lifestyle change, such as by embodying the art of stoicism and using it in your daily life, one of the most valuable things that you can do for yourself is to continue studying that change indefinitely. For stoicism, this means that you want to continue studying the history of stoicism, what stoicism actually is, and how modern stoicism works so that you can begin applying that knowledge in your life more consistently. Ongoing education around lifestyle changes is one of the most powerful things that you can gift yourself with if you are truly serious about making permanent changes in your life.

The first reason why you want to continue educating yourself on these changes is that the more you know, the easier it is for you to actually apply the goal of stoicism into your life. As you continue to read more books, listen to podcasts, read blogs, and otherwise consume information about stoicism, you gain more insight as to how it can be applied in a variety of different experiences or situations that you may encounter in your life. As a result, you can more clearly understand how it works, what it means, and what it looks like in practical application. This means that when you encounter times that may be more trying on your emotions, you can start moving through the process of adapting to a more stoic approach easier.

Another reason why ongoing education is powerful is that it gives you a more dynamic understanding of what stoicism actually is. Every single person who has ever written on stoicism and who will ever write on it will approach the subject slightly different from everyone else who has approached the subject. This is because we all have slightly different interpretations of what stoicism is, why it is important, and how it should be applied into everyday life. As you continue educating yourself on how stoicism is being applied by other people, you can educate yourself on how you can further personalize it for your own experience as well. You may find that what has worked in the modern application of stoicism for others either fits great with you or does not resonate so much and you need to pursue a different understanding to help you achieve more.

As well, your deeper understanding of the core foundation of what stoicism is will help you begin to develop your own ideas around what it truly means and why it relates to your personal beliefs on life itself. In this way, your ongoing education around stoicism can stimulate you to begin formulating your own opinions and perspectives and even further embodying it into your own life in a way that genuinely fits you and your needs. Through this type of personalized embodiment, you grow a closer and more intimate connection to your practice which makes it easier for you to commit and devote to it in your life.

Lastly, your ongoing education around stoicism will keep it relevant to you. In a society where our average attention span is about 2.5 seconds long, it is not uncommon to read a great book, feel inspired, and then completely forget about everything you learned just a few days later. If you truly want to embody everything that stoicism has to offer, you need to be willing to stay devoted to your practice and continue keeping it at the forefront of your life. You need to put in the continued attention and effort into understanding what it is and deepening your connection with it so that you can keep growing and advancing alongside stoicism. Otherwise, there is a good chance that you will simply forget or it will become unimportant to you, and you will lack the ability to embody stoicism in your life.

Endurance Training

The last thing that you need to begin implementing into your life when it comes to achieving stoicism is developing an endurance. This endurance can be developed by regularly strengthening the foundation of your entire lifestyle change through consistent mental toughness building. The more you work towards increasing your mental strength and toughness, the stronger your foundation will be and the easier it will be for you to maintain your stoic lifestyle. If you let your mental toughness foundation break down, the rest of your practices are going to break down alongside it, and you are going to struggle to really embody stoicism in your life. That is why we started with mental toughness training and the practices that you need to begin embodying to develop the mental strength and resiliency that you need to succeed.

I suggest that you spend several minutes per day purposefully working towards building your mental toughness. You can do this by scheduling aside time for practicing the practices given to you in <u>Chapter 2: Mental Toughness – Maintaining Your Mental Toughness in Challenging Times</u>, as well as by practicing them spontaneously when they are particularly useful in life, such as when you are going through a hard time. Practicing mental toughness on a regular basis is going to help you stay strong enough to continue choosing your rational thinking mind over your emotional thinking mind during trying times, which will keep you in alignment with stoicism.

If you are having a particularly challenging time building your mental toughness, I suggest you slow down and stay focused on your mental endurance for a while. Do not push yourself into advancing into the stoic disciplines until you have developed a deeper sense of mental toughness. Although you will likely generate some success in these disciplines, if you lack mental toughness, you may see the back-and-forth of success-then-setbacks as too much and may find yourself feeling like you would rather give up than continue. This might completely throw your entire game off, which can destroy your success and leave you feeling defeated before you ever really got the chance to begin.

Instead, take your time and really focus on building a strong foundation of mental toughness first so that your disciplines are far easier for you to uphold. When your mental toughness is developed enough that you can see the benefits of your resiliency and personal strength, then you can begin moving on to developing your disciplines as they will be much easier to develop and maintain.

In addition to building your mental toughness through mental practices, I would also suggest that you begin building a physical endurance practice as well. Physical endurance will not only support you in maintaining your health, which is an important element of stoicism, but it will also help you build mental endurance as well. Physical endurance requires a high degree of mental commitment and devotion, which is what makes it so powerful in developing your mental endurance. Furthermore, the number of challenges that you will face physically in building your endurance will teach you about just how strong you are when it comes to emotional endurance, too.

Chapter 6: Daily Application of Stoicism

Finally, you have reached the point where you can begin applying stoicism into your everyday life! At this point, you have a strong enough understanding of stoicism and all of the tools in place for you to begin developing stoicism in your life, so you are now ready to begin developing daily practices for stoicism. This is where you really get to let your practice until now shine through as you get to put the "final touches" of your lifestyle change into place. Through these daily practices, you are going to really begin to see the fruits of your labors as these practices are small yet consistent, so they pack a big punch in making real changes in your life.

In this chapter, we are going to discuss **14 ways that you can begin applying stoicism into your daily life**. This may sound like a lot, but in reality, many of these practices are simply about mindset shifts that you can focus on creating and embodying every single day. As you do, the shifts of stoicism in your life will begin to manifest rapidly as your consistent application of stoic practices begins to snowball into your successful growth. So, if you are ready to finally apply stoicism into your everyday life, let's start!

Knowing Your True Freedom

The first way that you can begin embodying stoicism in your everyday life is by generating perspective around where your freedom lies and how your freedom can be achieved. Epictetus, a Greek stoic philosopher, once quoted that "No man is free who is not a master of himself." In other words, the only true way to gain freedom is to understand yourself and begin mastering yourself regarding your emotions, your reactions, and the way that you decide to live your life. Remember, of all the things that exist in this world, the only thing that you truly have any control over is yourself. When you learn how to control yourself, you experience true freedom because you learn how to end your suffering in any circumstance that you may face.

Whenever you are faced with trying situations in your life, recognize what your instinctive reaction is and pause for a moment to hold back from that immediate reaction. Instead, slow yourself down and take the time to gather control over yourself and your emotions before proceeding. This way, you can proceed with control over your emotional passion and expression, thus allowing you to begin making conscious choices and avoiding the suffering of emotional reactions. As you do this, you begin to develop a sense of control over the way you move, the actions you take, and the way that you express your emotional self. This type of self-control and emotional constraint becomes your biggest ally when it comes to rationally moving through your life and making choices that genuinely serve your overall well-being. Through this, your life somewhat turns into a game of chess where every move is clearly thought out and, if moved correctly, can bring you that much closer to achieving your ultimate goal.

If you want to experience a better life, you need to take responsibility for your own growth and begin developing your skills around your personal growth. The more you take responsibility, the more you put yourself back in control over your own experiences and the greater you can grow in life. This pause can mean the difference between creating a new future or recreating an (ineffective) historical past.

The Circle of Influence and the Circle of Concern

One of the most powerful instruments that exist in stoicism is the circle of influence and the circle of concern. When you begin to study these two circles, you start to realize that everything in your life falls into two categories: things that you can control (your circle of influence) and things that you cannot control (your circle of concern.) The things within your circle of control or influence are things that you can actually make effective change in through your own personal choices. The things within your circle of concern are things that you cannot directly control and that you have to either accept *or* reframe using things that are within your circle of influence.

The things that fall within your circle of influence include things like: where you work, what you buy, what you read, what skills you choose to learn, what people you meet, what friends you keep in your life, and what your attitude towards life is. These are all things that you can personally control either by adjusting your mindset around them or by choosing to engage more or less with them. For that reason, these fall into your circle of influence because you can directly influence them in your life.

The things that fall into your circle of concern include things like: the news, the economy, the political views of other people, the weather, natural disasters, wars, other people's lives, and other people's opinions. These types of things are completely beyond your control, so you will never be able to influence them or change them directly. Instead, you need to decide to either accept them as they are or adjust the way that you perceive them in your life so that you can accept them. In the end, your only real option towards ending suffering around your circle of concern is to choose to change your perception around these things.

Reframing Your Attitude on Death

According to stoicism, the sooner you define how you feel about death, the less you are going to fear death, and the sooner you will begin enabling yourself to live a better life. As Socrates stated, "To fear death, my friends, is only to think ourselves wise, without being wise: for it is to think that we know what we do not know. For anything that men can tell, death may be the greatest good that can happen to them: but they fear it as if they knew quite well that it was the greatest of evils. And what is this but that shameful ignorance of thinking that we know what we do not know?" Death itself is something that many modern people fear, but the fear itself needs to be addressed if you are ever going to overcome it so that you can allow yourself to live truly. Often, the fear of death is derived from the fear of not living a great enough life before death happens, and as a result, people begin to fear what would happen if they died. The common worry is "What if I die and I did not live my best life?" which can naturally be overcome by actually choosing to live your life. However, if you are so afraid of dying that you refuse to start living, then you will always live in this fear of not living your best life because you let that very fear hold you back.

Death itself is inevitable, no matter what way you look at it, so choosing to fear it will only hold you back further. This does not mean that you have to look forward to or even welcome death, but choosing to overcome your intense fear around it will help you begin living a better life in general as you will no longer fear what could happen if you did die. Instead, you choose to come to peace with the fact that the end is coming just like you choose to come to peace with the fact that the past has already happened. As such, you move forward with a greater emphasis on *right now*.

If the fear of death is really prominent for you, rather than trying to combat your fear of death, you may find that your ability to overcome the fear is quite challenging. In this case, rather than attempting to terminate the fear itself, you may instead choose to begin reframing that fear. For example: what are you more afraid of, death or never having lived? What are you more afraid of, dying young with a great life of exciting memories or dying old with a life of regret and missed opportunities? What are you more afraid of, going out and dying in a tragic accident or never having exposed yourself to the joys of living in the first place? Do you get where I'm going with this? If you cannot completely overcome your fear of dying, make your fear of dying smaller than your fear of missing out on living.

Growing Comfortable in Discomfort

Life is filled with challenges no matter what way you choose to live your life. If you choose to sit still in your life, you are going to face the challenges of having to fight as hard as you can to avoid change and experience the pain of not growing. If you choose to grow with your life, you are going to face the challenges of obstacles that come with growth and the growing pains that are inevitable along the way. Either way, you are going to experience some degree of suffering in your life, no matter what you do. However, if you choose to endure the growing pains as they come, you can assure that they are going to be much less painful than the lifelong pain of trying to stop things from changing.

Think of your life as an old school game of Super Mario: the screen is moving and you have to keep moving with it, or else, it moves and you get left behind eventually. In the case of Super Mario, your character would simply die, and you would start again with a new life. In the case of real life, you are simply going to experience more and more pressure coming against you which will require you to grow stronger and stronger to prevent it from actually hitting you. In most cases, you will grow exhausted at some point and weeks, months, or even years of missed growth opportunities will crash upon you all at once and demand serious change from you. In this case, the pressure of waiting plus the pressure of being hit with all of your life lessons at once will produce way more suffering than growing at a natural rate would have.

Growing comfortable with discomfort now means that you will only ever have to endure manageable amounts of discomfort in your life. As long as you continue moving forward, that pressure will not build up, and you will never experience the need to hold a mountain over your head while praying that it doesn't crush you when it all falls down at once. The suffering that you experience when you choose to grow instead of standing still is far less than if you were to never change at all.

Recreating Yourself as a Person

Until now, you have likely held fairly tightly to the identity of who you are as a person. You probably have an identity that you have clung to all of your life, or at least for most of your life, that has been shaped by significant memories and experiences that you have shared with other people. Maybe the combination of your Mother telling you that you were too sensitive and you crying after being bullied off the high school basketball team has left you believing that you are too sensitive as a person. Maybe your Dad telling you that you are special and your teachers always putting unique stickers on your work has led you to believe that you are more special than those around you. Whatever your belief about yourself may be, you can guarantee that it is not accurate as to who you truly are.

Psychology says that there are three elements to our identity: how we experience the world, our inner voice, and our persona that we share with people around us. Each of these parts of our identity is slightly different from the other two parts of our identity, thus leaving us with our true identity falling somewhere in between these three moving parts. When you realize this to be true, you realize that not only has your belief around your identity been wrong all this time but also that you can completely recreate those beliefs and your identity within yourself.

As you embody the goals of stoicism in your own life, seek to learn how you can embody it in a way that truly changes who you are. Rather than being a person who is heavily driven by emotion or who engages in irrational behavior, become a person who is driven by rational thinking. Reinvent yourself as the person who is reliable, trustworthy, and stable. Begin to develop trust in yourself and learn how to rely on yourself as being the one person that you can turn to when you are in need of genuine change in your life. Start building your relationship with yourself and everything in your life will change.

Embodying Your Own Philosophies

Remember your philosophy journal? Now is a great time to begin digging into it and embodying everything that you have been writing inside of that journal, including your own philosophies on what life is and what it means. When you begin embodying your own philosophies in life, you begin to create an intimate and personal connection with life itself. Rather than simply embracing what someone else says is true and believes is right, you can start embracing what you believe to be true and right for you.

If you believe in stoicism, chances are that your personal philosophies and beliefs somehow connect to stoicism as well. So, not only will this help you live more in alignment with your personal truth, but it will also help you embody a deeper connection to the stoic way of life and embrace it in a more personalized manner. Choose what your purpose is in life, discover your mission, and choose to live in alignment with your purpose and mission every single day. Seek the opportunity to make your own life and the lives of those around you better through your actions and infuse your everyday living with your purpose and mission.

When you embody your own philosophies, you not only start living life on your own terms, but you also start distributing your own knowledge and understanding more powerfully. What if people like Epictetus, Zeno, and Socrates never shared their philosophies in life with those around them? Had this never happened, the Greek school of philosophy would have never been established and stoicism, amongst many other philosophies, would have never come into existence. It does not serve to keep your beliefs and philosophies to yourself when they can serve better when they are being shared with the world around you.

Always Work Towards Your Personal Mission

One of the goals of stoicism is to always be working towards achieving your personal mission in life. When you have identified what it is that you truly want to achieve with your life and what purpose you serve here on earth, choosing how to respond to challenging situations becomes a lot easier. With a clear vision, you can see what it is that you are working towards and you know exactly what you need to factor in when it comes to choosing the reasonable solution to move forward with. This makes navigating emotional challenges more manageable because you know what it is that you are working towards, so there is more at stake if you *don't* manage your emotions and respond stoically.

As you grow, your goals and dreams are going to change in your life, but your mission is always going to stay the same. Your mission is what it is that you want to achieve in your life overall, and it tends to remain consistent throughout your goals and your dreams. When you consistently work towards an overall mission in your life, it becomes easier for you to know yourself and handle yourself in virtually any situation that you face even unexpected or challenging ones. You automatically start considering your mission and that which matters most to you in the face of challenges and rationally thinking about how you can honor your mission and work in alignment with it while still proceeding. In the goal of stoicism, this prevents irrational emotional outbursts because you know what it is that you desire to achieve, so you are not caught in emotional turmoil with no clear understanding as to what is causing it or why. Instead, you can easily tell which of your primary missions or values has been compromised or is being threatened by the situation at hand, and you can rationally choose action steps that will help you proceed in alignment with your mission.

Be a Student of Life

Seneca, a Roman stoic philosopher, once said: "As long as you live, keep learning how to live." Being able to recognize that you are never going to know all that there is to know about life is imperative in allowing yourself to always remain open to all that life has to offer you. If you want to live your best life, you need to live a life with humility by realizing that you will always be learning, as long as you are alive. Every day will present you with new challenges, opportunities, changes, and lessons. As long as you are willing to, you can awaken to these lessons and embrace them and learn how to implement them so that each day is better than the last.

You may think that some days have nothing to teach you or find yourself feeling as though sometimes it isn't *you* who needs to embrace the lessons being presented. Trust that any time you attempt to push the responsibility onto someone else, you are not paying attention to life with an open enough mind because you are allowing your ego and emotions to cloud your judgment. You need to be willing to admit that the lessons being presented in life are also being presented to you.

If you find that you are genuinely going through your days with nothing to learn, your lesson may be that you need to challenge yourself more. Seek opportunities to learn and grow and put yourself in circumstances where you can start embracing greater challenges in your life. You may feel that being free of challenges is a blessing, but in reality, it is a sign that you are either ignorant towards everything around you or you are not doing enough to present yourself with growth opportunities.

Use this as an opportunity to take responsibility for yourself and your personal growth and well-being and create your reality in a new and exciting way.

Create Happiness, Don't Dream of It

One of the biggest teachings in stoicism is that your goal is not to dream of having happiness, but to create it instead. Rather than placing your happiness into worldly things like materialism, place the development of your happiness into yourself. According to Epictetus, the less you need to be happy, the happier you are going to be because fewer conditions will need to be met for your happiness to be achieved. Learning how to master your mind is a profound way to begin generating your own happiness and taking responsibility for your own contentment.

Happiness in and of itself is an illusion; it is merely an emotion that we experience just like anger and jealousy. When you realize this, you realize that just like anger or jealousy, happiness can be triggered by small things as well. This reality means that it does not need to be so challenging for you to experience happiness and that there are no certain circumstances that need to be met for you to be happy. Stop telling yourself things like "I will be happy when I have more money" or "I will be happier when I live in a new house", and instead, start realizing that you can be happy *right now*.

Beyond creating your own happiness, learn how to create your own contentment. Happiness, like other emotions, will come and go, so developing an attachment to living in a state of happiness can be challenging in and of itself. It can make the pursuit of happiness so cumbersome that you find that you truly cannot experience happiness at all and so, you are endlessly chasing something that you simply cannot catch. Instead, realize that in some situations, you are not going to be happy, and being content is just as pleasant as being happy, as it means that you are at peace with all that surrounds you and all that you embody.

Learn How to Be Present

The power of presence has been talked about a lot in the self-help industry over the past few years, but the reality is that presence is not a new concept nor is it one that was modernized by recent trends. Instead, the power of presence is something that has been talked about and taught about for years, including all the way back in ancient Greek times where stoicism was originally developed. That being said, the modern trends in the self-help industry means that learning about the art of presence and how to practice being in the moment is widely taught about and easy to educate yourself on.

The ability to remain present is something that needs to be addressed differently for different people. The reality is that not everyone is going to have the same thought processes or approaches to their realities in the same way, which means that everyone is going to need to hear the information in a particular way for it to actually *click*. That being said, do not shy away from reading and consuming all of the materials that you need to consume around presence to help you learn about what it means and how to embody presence in your own life. In fact, fully immerse yourself in the practice because once you get it, everything will absolutely change.

When you live your life in the present moment, forgiving the past and seeing everything as a new experience is effortless because you are in *this* moment, not one that has already passed you by or one that has yet to arrive. This means that your emotions attached to previous memories and challenges in your life no longer drive you through current experiences, which prevents you from responding to things with an excess of emotional passion. For example, if your spouse forgets to change the toilet paper roll, you do not feel compelled to get angry at him/her for the past three years of things that he/she had done wrong in your eyes over one isolated incident. Instead, you recognize that it was one isolated incident you can treat it as such, without the intense emotional response that you may instinctively attempt to respond with if you are still living in the past.

Always Take 100% Responsibility for Yourself

Learning how to take responsibility for yourself is not only a way to eliminate your suffering but is also a way to promote your growth and success in life, too. When you take responsibility for yourself, you put the control of your life back into your own hands and give yourself the tools that you need to heal, grow, and change throughout life. It may feel difficult, but when you take responsibility for yourself, you take responsibility for your feelings and your behaviors, and you give yourself exactly all of the power you need to make changes in your life.

From a perspective of looking back on your past, taking responsibility means that you take ownership for any role that you may have played in any challenges that you may have faced and that you recognize that you could have done things differently. Then, it means accepting yourself for the choices you made and realizing that you did your best with the knowledge that you had. For the challenges you faced that you could not have changed, you take responsibility for the feelings that you continue to face and the way that this may continue challenging you now in your present life. By taking this type of fierce responsibility for yourself, you give yourself the power that you need to change your life by healing, accepting, and moving on from your past.

From a present and futuristic standpoint, taking responsibility for yourself means accepting the behaviors and actions that you are taking right now in your everyday life and how they are impacting you right now and the future version of yourself. This means taking responsibility for the fact that when you do things such as wake up late, you face the consequences of being late to your engagements. This means taking responsibility for the fact that when you do things such as consistently show up late, you set your future self-up for failure by making it nearly impossible for you to hold down a job or earn an income. When you take responsibility for yourself, it means that you are taking responsibility for every single thing that you do or do not do and how it impacts you now and the future version of yourself that is yet to come.

If you truly want to live in alignment with the goals of stoicism you need to be willing to take responsibility for your personal growth, your emotional intelligence, and your ability to develop your rational thinking. You need to be willing to identify areas in your life where you could improve, and then actually take action necessary in moving forward and improving your life. When you take responsibility for yourself and your behaviors, it is like giving yourself the keys to your brand new life, and you have the choice to either make it something truly amazing for yourself.

Grow Beyond Materialism

Mahatma Gandhi once quoted, "Increase of material comforts, it may be generally laid down, does not in any way whatsoever conduce to moral growth." Materialism is an attitude that can produce a significant amount of suffering in anyone's life. Materialism is a constant source of stress in many modern societies where the mindset of "more, more, more" is basically bred into people from the beginning and is continuously injected into people's minds. In Western society, people are taught that they need to purchase new things on a constant basis to keep up with everything else. Fashion, housewares, trendy toys or gadgets, and many other consumerism-style products are constantly being produced and marketed to people through the power of emotions. Marketers market to people knowing that they want to fit in, be cool, enhance social status, experience happiness, or experience the sentimental or nostalgic value that the object may be able to offer. Of course, true consistent emotional happiness and support does not come from materialistic items, so it leads to people constantly going through cycles of buying things for joy and then feeling empty when the novelty wears off. As they say, the best things in life are not things.

Rather than exposing yourself to this suffering and being captivated by your emotions that fear being left behind or ridiculed for not having the latest and greatest things, learn how to deny materialism in your life. Purchase only what you need and what you genuinely desire, and leave everything else behind. Base your emotions on things that you can control, such as your thoughts and behaviors, and not on things that you can acquire like toys and fashion accessories. This way, you always feel truly in control over your emotional well-being, and you do not feel as though you are constantly at the mercy of corporations that are profiting off of your emotional instabilities.

Be of Service to Others

True love is a powerful thing, and with it can come experiences such as true joy, true contentment, true fulfillment, and true excitement. When you experience true love in your life, it opens up a world of other opportunities that you can enjoy through that love directly. It does not only open it up for you, but it opens it up for those around you as well, who are being loved through your service. Through this, a significant amount of pain and suffering ends because you are opening yourself and others up to a world of love and gentleness. Studies have shown that when you express love and kindness to one person, it often creates a ripple effect as they then express it to someone else, and the act carries on over many people.

In life, one of the greatest things that we can do for ourselves and for others is to serve. If you put anyone in the position of being able to serve genuinely, they will always say that they feel infinitely happier and more abundant as a result of their service. At the end of the day, we are always trying to serve someone in addition to ourselves: our family members, our friends, our audiences, our coworkers, or our employees. Some people make it their life mission to serve as many people as possible, whereas others are perfectly content just serving a small number of people in their lives. No matter what, though, if you ask anyone about what is important to them, some form of service will virtually always come to their mind.

We feel best when we serve because the act of giving love aligns us with the act of receiving love, and that genuinely feels good. When you can rationally think about how love improves your life and the lives of those around you in this way and act in a rational way around love, your ability to serve and generate true sustainable love increases. As a result, your suffering decreases and your genuine overall happiness grows.

Embody the Lighter Side of Life

There is nothing humble about living a life that is overwhelmed with seriousness. Just because the goal of stoicism is to be rational and reasonable does not mean that you are not able to experience humor and comedy in your life. In fact, one of the best ways that you can grow mental toughness and develop your stoicism is by learning how to make light of challenging situations. Seeing the brighter side of things and allowing yourself to embody the lightness helps you overcome the suffering that is attached with being too serious all of the time.

People who are too serious take things personally, feel the weight of the world on their shoulders, and struggle to let go and experience true joy and happiness in their lives. They find themselves feeling trapped in the energy of seriousness, and it can weigh them down and leave them feeling pessimistic in the long run. Not knowing how to laugh and see and embody the lighter side of life is just as damaging on your soul as never allowing yourself to overcome the suffering that you have endured in your life until now.

Learn how to laugh at yourself when you make mistakes, and laugh at the irony of challenging situations when you cannot overcome them with ease. Learn how to see life as something that is light and joyful, and discover how you can smile at the things that are beyond your control. Give yourself the gift of being gentle in your perspective and your opinion, and avoid trying to make everything so heavy and overwhelming all of the time. In seeing the lighter side of life, you give yourself the ability to avoid getting weighed down by seriousness, and you start enjoying yourself once again. Rather than holding you back and keeping you feeling overwhelmed, your emotions instead become an ally that helps you lead a greater life when you learn how to experience the lighter side of life itself.

Conclusion

You have officially read the entirety of *Stoicism: A Practical Guide for Beginners to Practice Stoicism: Complete Guide of Self-Discipline, Mental Toughness, Productivity, and Mastering Confidence, Jealousy, and Anger Management, and Everything You Need to Know About Stoicism*! Thanks for making it through to end of this guidebook. Let's hope it was informative and able to provide you with all of the tools you need to achieve your goals whatever they may be.

By now, you should have a strong understanding of what stoicism is, where it stems from, and how it has evolved to serve the modern world. Stoicism is a powerful art that, when appropriately applied, can help you master one of the most valuable tools that evolution has granted us: your rational mind. By applying the lessons that were taught to us by ancient Greek and Roman philosophers, you can discover powerful ways to move through your challenges and experience greater success in your personal, social, and professional lives. Through the proper application of stoic ways of life, not only can you find the opportunity to experience greater success, but you can also help your own personal evolution along. The more you refine and harness the power of your rational mind, the more you work in alignment with the very nature of being a human being. As a result, you can tap into the entire power of the human mind and experience more of just about everything you desire out of life.

Stoicism is a powerful lifestyle that teaches you about the importance of reducing your own personal suffering through embodying an ethical way of living that values high moral standards. When you embody stoicism, you teach yourself how to harness the power of your emotions and use them to inspire yourself to respond to things with a more rational approach. Through this rational approach, you can work towards effectively achieving the goals that your emotions had in the first place without the unnecessary implication of further suffering.

Despite how far we have evolved, humans continue to find themselves falling into the temptation of satisfying their emotions immediately and suffering for that satisfaction in the long run rather than managing their emotions effectively and benefiting overall. Stoicism continues to support us in overcoming this need for instant gratification by encouraging us to embody the pillars of high moral standards and ethical living by favoring our reasonable mind over our emotional one. This does not mean that you should be ignoring or avoiding your emotions, but instead that you should be working in alignment with your nature and discovering how you can move forward with a whole approach.

As you move forward from this book, continue working on building your mental toughness and resiliency so that you can experience a stronger foundation to build your practice of stoicism upon. Teach yourself how to stay dedicated by staying consistent in educating yourself about stoicism and developing a personal practice that aligns with your stoic development, too. In the early stages, you may benefit from keeping this handy so that you can refer back to Chapter 6: Daily Applications of Stoicism and inspire yourself to embody stoicism on a daily basis. At least, early on, this chapter will be handy in reminding you about how simply you can apply it in your everyday life. From learning to manage your anger at work more effectively so that you can continue to carry yourself in a productive way to learning how to accept your family and friends as they are and choosing to love them anyway, stoicism will help in many ways. The more you practice, the more this empowered way of living will have the capacity to change your complete life.

I encourage you as well to really take advantage of using your own philosophy diary where you, too, can begin discovering what life means to you and what you feel your purpose in life is. As you continue looking into your own inner studies, developing your personal mission, and sticking to it through your rational, decision-making becomes easier. In no time, you will discover just how easy it is to stick to the power of rational thinking when you have a genuine and powerful reason that inspires you to do so.

Lastly, if you enjoyed this audiobook I ask that you please take the time to review it on Audible.com. Your honest feedback would be greatly appreciated.

Thank you for listening.

Now, I would like to share with you a free sneak peek to another one of my books that I think you will really enjoy. The book is called "Emotional intelligence 2.0: A Practical Guide for Beginners" Published by Travis Goleman and Daniel Greaves. It's A Practical Guide that will teach you to master Social Intelligence, Emotional Awareness and Relationship Management. You will also learn How to use Conversational Skills to Persuade and Influence People.

Enjoy!

Introduction

You have heard so much about emotional intelligence that your interest is piqued. Whether you are a top-management official at work or a stay-at-home mom, emotional intelligence is important in your life. I commend you for taking the steps to develop your emotional intelligence skills. By doing so, you will only improve your quality of life from how you feel about yourself to how you feel about others, and ultimately, how others feel about you.

I can do all that just by reading this book, you may ask? Yup! You sure can.

The following chapters will discuss how you can develop your ability to master emotional intelligence and to see great improvements in your personal and professional life. The book is divided into 6 easy-to-read chapters that will give you insight into how to manage your emotional intelligence.

The first chapter will give a brief overview of what emotional intelligence is. Then the subsequent chapters will break down the tenets of emotional intelligence into more detail. Chapter 2 builds on Chapter 1 and explores what emotional intelligence looks like in your everyday life. From this chapter, we dive right into building skills that will help you improve your emotional intelligence. In Chapter 3, how to manage your emotions will be discussed, followed by how to improve your self-awareness in Chapter 4. Chapter 5 explains how to use social awareness and relationship management respectively.

At the end of every chapter, there will be a special section dedicated to giving you skills on how to develop each skill in order to become better at emotional intelligence. Also, please note that throughout the chapters, you will learn about Valerie who does not have an idea about emotional intelligence and her socially bankrupt life reflects it. Please do not be like Valerie!

Hopefully, by the end of this book, you will learn a lot from Valerie on what to do and what not to do in regards to emotional intelligence. At the end of the chapter, bullet points of the chapter topics and activities you can do to help develop your emotional intelligence will be given. Take small baby steps and do not be afraid to feel awkward as you try to implement the changes associated with emotional intelligence into your life. Every journey must start with one step and it is difficult before it gets easier. By the time you finish, you will notice how much your life has improved just because you decided to take the step to be more emotionally intelligent.

There are plenty of books on this subject on the market, so thanks again for choosing this one! Every effort was made to ensure it is full of as much useful information as possible. Please enjoy!

Chapter 1: What is Emotional Intelligence?

Meet Valerie. Valerie is a typical American who is married with two kids, a house, and a white picket fence. Oh yeah, she has a beautiful black Labrador as well. Valerie would consider her to have an average level of emotional intelligence. She does ok at work. Her familial, personal, and professional relationships are so-so. She feels like she's walking through life. Not going fast or slow, but just regular shmegular. She doesn't always feel in control and sometimes has panic attacks because she is overwhelmed, stressed, and unhealthy. She figures everyone else is going through the same things so it is not a big problem.

Cut to one busy day where Valerie is rushing to work because she has not communicated to her family members that she needs help and all of the chores and housework falls on her. Not too mention, she had to stay late at work the night before because she is a people pleaser which made her oversleep in the first place. Picture Valerie in a car, speeding down the highway in the rain before she hydroplanes smack dab into an eighteen-wheeler. Her car spins out of control and Valerie finds herself pinned behind her steering wheel in her car that is sideways in a ditch. Of course, a Good Samaritan saw the incident and immediately called emergency services who rushed to the scene. After the paramedics help her out the car, she is whisked to the hospital.

The good news is, she was alive. The bad news is, she has amnesia and she has to learn everything all over again. Facts like her children's names, her husband's name, and her dog's name will be seemingly easy to learn. However, the nuances of emotional intelligence seemed much more difficult to learn.

She has to learn how to identify her personal emotions, manage them when reacting to other people, as well as managing her social settings and relationships. Whew! Valerie is on a quest to relearn what emotional intelligence is, but Valerie is not alone. There are a lot of people who want to learn how to be emotionally intelligent and are on the same path as Valerie.

This book attempts to help people like Valerie and the readers navigate the tricky, topsy-turvy, abstract world of emotions and the unspoken rules that come with it. Unlike Valerie who is starting with a blank slate, most people have some type of experience with their emotions whether they have anger issues, are people pleasers, or are narcissists. Emotional intelligence draws upon your personal preferences and experiences to figure out how to survive in the world. In order to improve upon one's emotional intelligence, one must first understand what emotional intelligence is.

So what is emotional intelligence? Known in short as EI, emotional intelligence is the multi-faceted capacity of being in tune with your personal thoughts and emotions and being able to manage them in your daily living and in your dealings with other people. In order to be emotionally intelligent, you must first have mastery of who you are and know how to handle your emotions. Then you must know how to navigate relationships with other people, especially how to interpret and understand their emotions and how to be savvy in the way you respond to their emotions for optimal results. In other words, to be emotionally intelligent, you need to know what to say, when to say it, and how to say it. Sounds like a lot? You're right. Becoming emotionally intelligent can be overwhelming, but it is not impossible. It is a skill that can be learned with practice. Being emotionally intelligent is a trait many want to acquire because research has shown that emotionally intelligent people are deemed better leaders, better friends, and better family members. People with emotional intelligence do not necessarily have the highest IQ, but they understand how people work. As a result, their acumen in dealing with people helps them to be successful in a way that people who are not emotionally intelligent are not able to achieve.

Emotional intelligence was brought to the mainstream in 1995 by Daniel Goleman when he wrote the book *Emotional Intelligence: Why It Can Matter More Than IQ*. This book was seminal in changing how people thought about the power of emotions. Before this book, emotions were not seen as powerful tools to help you succeed. Emotions were seen as a hindrance. Goldman brought the importance of being emotionally intelligent to the forefront, but it was not an idea that originated with him. Way back in the day, over 2,000 years ago, Plato wrote that "All learning has an emotional base." Even though Plato had said that emotions were important centuries earlier, scientists did not always see it that way. However, in the 1920s, the idea that emotions were important re-emerged when Edward Thorndike named the ability to get along with others as "social intelligence."

In 1950, Abraham Maslow sparked the human potential movement and wrote about the importance of people enhancing their mental, physical, emotional, and spiritual strengths. From his research, lots of similar movements were launched and people began to build on his ideas. From this birth of new knowledge, two researchers, Peter Salovey and John "Jack" Mayer in the 1990s, have been credited with first using the term 'emotional intelligence.' In the article, Salovey and Mayer defined emotional intelligence as scientifically testable "intelligence." This work set the foundation for Daniel

Goleman's book in 1995. From there, many different offshoots of emotional intelligence were developed. For the purpose of this book, we will focus on emotional intelligence as being composed of four different parts consisting of self-management, self-awareness, social awareness, and relationship management.

Self-awareness is being in tune with your emotions. If you are self-aware, you are great at identifying and deciphering your emotions and using them effectively when you react to a situation. Self-management is the act of managing your emotions and the reactions to any situation you may find yourself in. The word 'manage' is key in the definition of self-management. If you are great at self-management, it does not mean that you do not get angry or experience emotions at all. It means that you are adept at how you manage those emotions to get the outcome you want. Social awareness is being keen to the social environment around you. And relationship management is all about handling your relationships whether they be professional, personal, or even the relationship with yourself. In later chapters, each separate component will be delved into in greater detail.

To understand how one learns about emotional intelligence, a person must understand how our brains work. Our brain is divided into three separate parts — the basal ganglia, limbic system, and neocortex. The basal ganglia are at the root of our brain and it is considered the place where all our instincts reside. When you feel something in your gut, the information travels directly to this region of your brain without going through the other regions. This is information that you do not have to think about at all. The next part of the brain is the limbic system. The information processed by this part of your brain is considered to be processed on the subconscious level.

Subconscious level information is a step above unconscious information and that information is right below our level of awareness. The subconscious level is where our emotions reside. It stores information about experiences good and bad that affect our behaviors, as well as it stores our value judgments. The neocortex is the next part of the brain. It controls your level of awareness. The information in this part of the brain is able to be accessed at will. It controls our reasoning, language, and thoughts. This brief overview of the brain is helpful to understand because certain activities suggested later on in the book target certain aspects of the brain. It is a cool tidbit to understand how the activities strengthen certain aspects of your brain so you can learn how to control your emotional intelligence better and be more aware.

Emotionally Intelligent Character Traits

How does someone who is emotionally intelligent act? People who are emotionally intelligent normally have a few characteristics that let others know they are emotionally intelligent individuals.

- Emotionally intelligent people have empathy. They are able to understand how others are feeling in any given situation. In other words, like the cliché says, emotionally intelligent people are able to walk in someone else's shoes. They are able to understand how someone with a sick child may be having a rough time or understand the importance of being nice to everyone whether they have experienced that situation or not.

- Emotional intelligent people also think deeply about their emotions and other people's emotions – a lot. They are pros at knowing how to relate and manipulate to other people in order to get the best outcome possible.

- Emotionally intelligent people do not run from criticism. They are able to take feedback easily without being defensive. They are able to take what people say about them, dissect the criticism, and take from the criticism what they may.

- Emotionally intelligent people are also genuine people. They seek authenticity in their relationships with other people and tend to see the best in people. Hence, they also are able to forgive and forget slights against them rather easily.

- People who are emotionally intelligent are very positive. They are not angels. However, they are effective at refocusing their thoughts, so they do not act impulsively and do something that they will regret later.

- Emotionally intelligent people do not run from confrontation. They face the criticism head-on and then go from there. They handle the conflict with ease, even if their egos are wounded in the process.

- Emotionally intelligent people are excellent communicators. They know their personality type and communication style and are able to effectively communicate with others and know the style in which they prefer to be communicated.

People who are not emotionally intelligent tend to be the exact opposite.

- They are easily flustered and easily angered.

- They are selfish and they only care about one person - themselves.

- They do not think before they speak and they talk all the time without any care to how other people may react to what they are saying.

- People who are not emotionally intelligent are usually not the easiest people to get along with.

Emotionally intelligent people are leagues ahead of people who are not emotionally intelligent. Interestingly, one can have characteristics of being emotionally intelligent and also have characteristics of not being emotionally intelligent. The key is to try and work on your emotional intelligence until you are competent in all four areas of being emotionally intelligent. This takes work.

For someone who has never ever thought about learning more about emotional intelligence, the information explained thus far may seem suspect. You may be one of the people who believe that emotional intelligence is a fluke. You may think that it is not necessary or important to be in tune with your emotions or in tune with the emotions of others in order to be a better person. You may think emotional intelligence is nothing but hippy-dippy foolery that has no place in the same sentence with rational thought. You may think that emotional intelligence has no effect on your success. However, think of that one person that you would not rather be around. This person always makes inappropriate jokes. They never know what to say. It is like they always have a foot in their mouth.

These types of people have no self-awareness. No one wants to be around them. This is why emotional intelligence matters. There is no black-and-white version of emotional intelligence.

It is possible that you are good with some of the aspects of emotional intelligence and you need help controlling the other aspects. Perhaps you are good at knowing your feelings and you're able to manage your emotions, but you are terrible at communicating with others. Hence, your relationship management needs work. Perhaps you are excellent at navigating relations and social settings, whether they are professional or personal because you are great at putting on a front but your personal life is in shambles. You may need to work on your self-awareness. Or perhaps, you can easily be wonderful at managing other people's relationships. You can be the one friend that everyone comes to when they need help, but you are horrible at your own self-management. It happens. Just because you are okay with three out of the four aspects of emotional intelligence does not mean that you cannot improve the other aspects. Wanting to be aware of how emotional intelligence works is commendable and there are definitely skills and exercises that you can do to improve each and every aspect of your emotional intelligence core.

Yet, emotional intelligence can have a dark side. There are some people who are master manipulators. They are so good at emotional intelligence that they can draw upon what someone else is feeling in order to get the outcome that they want. These people know how to pit people against each other, play the victim, and play on people's emotions to remain in control at all times. If you are not emotionally intelligent, you can really fall victim to their traps rather quickly. One of the most important reasons for developing your emotional intelligence is to be a better person and to protect yourself against people who have nefarious intentions.

Lucky for Valerie, she is starting with a blank slate when learning how to develop her emotional intelligence. She does not have to be concerned about all the baggage that comes with learning a new skill. For her, she has to begin by learning what emotional intelligence is. So buckle up. The next chapter will go into more detail about how emotional intelligence affects our daily life whether we are aware of it or not.

Chapter Highlights

- Emotional intelligence was coined by Daniel Goleman in 1995 by his book *Emotional Intelligence: Why It Is More Important Than Your IQ*.
- Emotional Intelligence is composed of four different parts — self-management, self-awareness, social awareness, and relationship management.
- Our brain is composed of three regions that control our thoughts and emotions. By doing exercises to improve every aspect of our brain, one can improve their emotional intelligence.

Do the Work

- Why are you interested in learning more about emotional intelligence? Is it to improve personally or is it to improve in a professional setting or is it another reason? Knowing why you want to learn about emotional intelligence can help you when you get to a difficult spot in your learning.

- Do you think that you have more traits of being emotionally intelligent or more traits of not being emotionally intelligent?
- Emotional intelligence is composed of four different components — self-awareness, self-management, social awareness, and relationship management. Which component do you think you need to work on?
- Before emotional intelligence was brought to the forefront, there was a philosopher who said that "emotions are at the base of every decision?" Who was it?

Thank you, this preview is now over.

I hope you enjoyed this preview of my book Emotional Intelligence: Understand Your Emotions and Create Profound Relationships by Frank Steven.

Please make sure to check out the full book on Amazon.com

Thank you.

STOICISM COLLECTION: THE MOST INSPIRING STOIC QUOTES

Powerful Stoic Quotes About Self-Discipline, Mental Toughness, Perseverance, Emotional Freedom, Self-Confidence, and Goal Setting

Congratulations on purchasing Stoicism Quotes book and thank you for doing so!

This book will be all about the most important quotes from famous stoic figures which will give you the wisdom and knowledge needed in your day to day life. This will help you especially if you are experiencing hardships and shortcomings. We will go over the different stoicism quotes that are carefully chosen to overcome your challenges whatever they a
re. The content in this book will guide you along the way and help you to attain a good mental stability.

Thanks again for choosing us. Every effort was made to ensure it is full of as much useful content as possible. Please enjoy!

Table of Contents

Stoic quotes from Marcus Aurelius.................................... 108

Best Stoicism quotes from Seneca 117

Famous Stoicism Quotes from Epictetus 134

Famous Stoicism Quotes from Zeno of Citium 140

33 Various Quotes from Different Stoics............................. 143

Spiritual and philosophical quotes of stoic school 148

Stoic quotes from Marcus Aurelius

Before we start the quotes, here is a quick introduction about who is Marcus Aurelius. Marcus Aurelius also called as the "Philosopher" has rise to power as a Roman Emperor in the year 161. He rules the Roman Empire along with his brother which is named as Lucius Verus, until the death of his brother in the year 169. Marcus Aurelius continued to rule as a Roman Emperor until his death in March 17, 180.

He was also known as one of the "Five Good Emperors" because of his good values and wisdom. Marcus Aurelius said to have at least 13 children with his wife Faustina (his first cousin) on their 30-year marriage.

He is also well-known for his several writings and one of them is called as the "Meditations" which is aimed for guiding people of self-improvement. Although the exact title of the work is still unknown but it is widely known as Meditation which is given when the writing is translated in modern English in the year 1792.

Marcus Aurelius Died in March 17, 180 because of natural causes in the city of Vindobona which is Vienna in today's world. He was buried in Hadrian's mausoleum until the Visigoth attack the city in the year 410. He died at the age of 58 years old.

Let's start with a selection of the best 61 Stoicism Quotes from the great influencer of Stoicism:

1.   "Think of the life you have lived until now as over and, as a dead man, see what's left as a bonus and live it according

to Nature. Love the hand that fate deals you and play it as your own, for what could be more fitting?"

2. "It never ceases to amaze me: we all love ourselves more than other people, but care more about their opinion than our own."

3. "In your actions, don't procrastinate. In your conversations, don't confuse. In your thoughts, don't wander. In your soul, don't be passive or aggressive. In your life, don't be all about business."

4. "If it is not right, do not do it, if it is not true, do not say it."

5. "The best revenge is not to be like your enemy."

6. "Waste no more time arguing what a good man should be. Be one."

7. "Choose not to be harmed — and you won't feel harmed. Don't feel harmed — and you haven't been."

8. "It's time you realized that you have something in you more powerful and miraculous than the things that affect you and make you dance like a puppet."

9. "External thinks are not the problem. It's your assessment of them. Which you can erase right now."

10. "If anyone can refute me—show me I'm making a mistake or looking at things from the wrong perspective—I'll gladly change. It's the truth I'm after, and the truth never harmed anyone."

11. "You could leave life right now. Let that determine what you do and say and think."

12. "Be tolerant with others and strict with yourself."

13. "If you are pained by any external thing, it is not this thing that disturbs you, but your own judgment about it. And it is in your power to wipe out this judgment now."

14. "Things stand outside of us, themselves by themselves, neither knowing anything of themselves nor expressing any judgment."

15. "The art of living is more like wrestling than dancing."

16. "It is not death that a man should fear, but he should fear never beginning to live."

17. "Loss is nothing else but change, and change is Nature's delight"

18. "Begin to begin is half the work, let half still remain; again begin this, and thou wilt have finished"

19. "A man's worth is no greater than his ambitions"

20. "Nothing happens to any man that he is not formed by nature to bear"

21. "There is nothing happens to any person but what was in his power to go through with"

22. "Anger cannot be dishonest."

23. "How much more grievous are the consequences of anger than the causes of it."

24. "Despise not death, but welcome it, for nature wills it like all else."

25. "Today I escaped from anxiety. Or no, I discarded it, because it was within me, in my own perceptions—not outside."

26. "[It is] like seeing roasted meat and other dishes in front of you and suddenly realizing: This is a dead fish. A dead bird. A dead pig. Or that this noble vintage [wine] is rotted grapes... perceptions like that... latching onto things and piercing through them, to see what they really are... to strip away the legend that encrusts them."

27. "Does what's happened keep you from acting with justice, generosity, self control, sanity, prudence, honesty, humility, straightforwardness, and all other qualities that allow a person's nature to fulfill itself? So remember this principle when something threatens to cause you pain: the thing itself was no misfortune at all; to endure it and prevail is great good fortune."

28. "Were you to live three thousand years, or even thirty thousand, remember that the sole life which a man can lose is that which he is living at the moment...he can have no other life than the one he loses. For the passing minute is every man's equal possession, but what has once gone by is not ours."

29. "Get rid of the judgment, get rid of the 'I am hurt,' you are rid of the hurt itself."

30. "Everything is right for me that is right for you, O Universe. Nothing for me is too early or too late that comes in due time for you. Everything is fruit to me that your seasons bring, O Nature. From you are all things, in you are all things, to you all things return."

31. "If you work at that which is before you, following right reason seriously, vigorously, calmly, without allowing anything else to distract you, but keeping your divine part pure, as if you were bound to give it back immediately; if you hold to this, expecting nothing, but satisfied to live now according to nature, speaking heroic truth in every word that you utter, you will live happy. And there is no man able to prevent this."

32. "How ridiculous and how strange is to be surprised at anything that happens in life!"

33. "Outward things cannot touch the soul, not in the least degree; nor have they admission to the soul, nor can they turn or move the soul; but the soul turns and moves itself alone."

34. "Because your own strength is unequal to the task, do not assume that it is beyond the powers of man; but if anything is within the powers and province of man, believe that it is within your own compass also"

35. "Or is it your reputation that's bothering you? But look at how soon we're all forgotten. The abyss of endless time that swallows it all. The emptiness of all those applauding hands. The people who praise us — how capricious they are, how arbitrary. And the tiny region in which it all takes place. The whole earth a point in space—and most of it uninhabited. How many people there will be to admire you, and who they are."

36. "If you are distressed by anything external, the pain is not due to the thing itself, but to your estimate of it; and this you have the power to revoke at any moment."

37. "Never let the future disturb you. You will meet it, if you have to, with the same weapons of reason which today arm you against the present."

38. "Misfortune nobly born is good fortune."

39. "Whatever happens, happens such as you are either formed by nature able to bear it, or not able to bear it. If such as you are by nature form'd able to bear, bear it and fret not: But if such as you are not naturally able to bear, don't fret; for when it has consum'd you, itself will perish. Remember, however, you are by nature form'd able to bear whatever it is in the power of your own opinion to make supportable or tolerable, according as you conceive it advantageous, or your duty, to do so."

40. "And here are two of the most immediately useful thoughts you will dip into. First that things cannot touch the mind: they are external and inert; anxieties can only come from your internal judgement. Second, hat all these things you see will change almost as you look at them, and then will be no more. Constantly bring to mind all that you yourself have already seen changed. The universe is change: life is judgement."

41. "Remember two things: i. that everything has always been the same, and keeps recurring, and it makes no difference whether you see the same things recur in a hundred years or two hundred, or in an infinite period; ii. that the longest lived and those who will die soonest lose the same thing. The present

is all that they can give up, since that is all you have, and what you do not have you cannot lose."

42. "You need to avoid certain things in your train of thought: everything random, everything irrelevant. And certainly everything self important or malicious. You need to get used to winnowing your thoughts, so that if someone says, "What are your thinking about?" you can respond at once (and truthfully) that you are thinking this or thinking that."

43. "When force of circumstance upsets your equanimity, lose no time in recovering your self control, and do not remain out of tune longer than you can help. Habitual recurrence to the harmony will increase your mastery of it."

44. "You have power over your mind—not outside events. Realize this, and you will find strength."

45. "Because a thing seems difficult for you, do not think it impossible for
anyone to accomplish."

46. "Here is a rule to remember in future, when anything tempts you to feel bitter: not 'This is misfortune', but 'To bear this worthily is good fortune.'"

47. "Do what you will. Even if you tear yourself apart, most people will continue doing the same things."

48. "Do not indulge in dreams of having what you have not, but reckon up the chief of the blessings you do possess, and then thankfully remember how you would crave for them if they were not yours."

49. "A key point to bear in mind: The value of attentiveness varies in proportion to its object. You're better off not giving the small things more time than they deserve."

50. "You have power over your mind   not outside events. Realize this, and you will find strength."

51. "Not to live as if you had endless years ahead of you. Death overshadows you. While you're alive and able -- be good.."

52. "Many of the anxieties that harass you are superfluous... Expand into an ampler region, letting your thought sweep over the entire universe."

53. "Plato has a fine saying, that he who would discourse of man should survey, as from some high watchtower, the things of earth."

54. "Remember: Matter. How tiny your share of it. Time. How brief and fleeting your allotment of it. Fate. How small a role you play in it."

55. "You can discard most of the junk that clutters your mind...and clear out space for yourself... by comprehending the scale of the world... by contemplating infinite time... by thinking of the speed with which things change—each part of every thing; the narrow space between our birth and death; the infinite time before; the equally unbounded time that follows."

56. "Asia and Europe: distant recesses of the universe. The ocean: a drop of water. Mount Athos: a molehill. The present: a split second in eternity. Minuscule, transitory, insignificant."

57. "The things you think about determine the quality of your mind."

58. "In a little while you will have forgotten everything; in a little while everything will have forgotten you. "

59. "Choose not to be harmed and you won't feel harmed. Don't feel harmed and you haven't been. "

60. "Very little is needed to make a happy life; it is all within yourself, in your way of thinking."

61. "If thou would'st master care and pain,
Unfold this book and read and read again
Its blessed leaves, whereby thou soon shalt see
The past, the present, and the days to be
With opened eyes; and all delight, all grief,
Shall be like smoke, as empty and as brief."

The quotes from Marcus Aurelius are now over. Let's now hear about Seneca's version of stoicism through 143 stoic quotes.

Best Stoicism quotes from Seneca

Before we start the quotes, here is a quick introduction about who is Seneca...

Seneca also known as "Seneca the Younger" or "Lucuius Annaeus Seneca" is best known for being a Roman philosopher, writer, statesman, and tutor/advisor of Emperor Nero.

He was born in the year 4 BCE in Cordoba in Hispania. He was well-known because of his philosophical works and for his plays, which are all based on tragedies. He has also written a lot of essays during his lifetime as well as 124 letters that deals with issues of morality.

He was known as a "tragedian" because of the genre of his works and the most notable works that he had are Medea and Thyestes.

He was later accused of arranging a plot to assassinate Nero and was forced to commit suicide by Emperor Nero. Most of the historian says that he was likely innocent of the accusations that was thrown upon him and all the accusations was because of his enemies in politics. His wife Pompeia Paulina was very sad and wanted to share the same fate with her husband Seneca but Nero ordered the soldiers to take a look at her and bandaged her to prevent her from killing herself. She died a few years later because of sickness and sadness.

Let's start with a selection of the best 143 Stoicism Quotes from Seneca, :

1. "We are more often frightened than hurt; and we suffer more in imagination than in reality."

2. "If a man knows not which port he sails, no wind is favorable."

3. "No person has the power to have everything they want, but it is in their power not to want what they don't have, and to cheerfully put to good use what they do have."

4. "Nothing, to my way of thinking, is a better proof of a well ordered mind than a man's ability to stop just where he is and pass some time in his own company."

5. "He who fears death will never do anything worth of a man who is alive."

6. "This is our big mistake: to think we look forward to death. Most of death is already gone. Whatever time has passed is owned by death."

7. "Life is very short and anxious for those who forget the past, neglect the present, and fear the future."

8. "I judge you unfortunate because you have never lived through misfortune. You have passed through life without an opponent—no one can ever know what you are capable of, not even you."

9. "How does it help...to make troubles heavier by bemoaning them?"

10. "People are frugal in guarding their personal property; but as soon as it comes to squandering tim ethey are most wasteful of the one thing in which it is right to be stingy."

11. "One of the most beautiful qualities of true friendship is to understand and to be understood."

12. "A gem cannot be polished without friction, nor a man perfected without trials."

13. "Wherever there is a human being, there is an opportunity for kindness."

14. "Life's like a play, it's not the length, but the excellence of the acting that matters."

15. "The day which we fear as our last is but the birthday of eternity."

16. "While we are postponing, life speeds by."

17. "When I think over what I have said, I envy dumb people."

18. "Consider, when you're enraged at any one, what you would probably think if he should die during the dispute."

19. "The things hardest to bear are sweetest to remember."

20. "When we are well, we all have good advice for those who are ill."

21. "Anger, if not restrained, is frequently more hurtful to us than the injury that provokes it."

22. "That is never too often repeated, which is never sufficiently learned."

23. "He that does good to another does good also to himself."

24. "There is nothing in the world so much admired as a man who knows how to bear unhappiness with courage."

25. "If you judge, investigate."

26. "No man enjoys the true taste of life, but he who is ready and willing to quit it."

27. "See how many are better off than you are, but consider how many are worse."

28. "The mind unlearns with difficulty what it has long learned."

29. "Whatever fortune has raised to a height, she has raised only to cast it down."

30. "Not how long, but how well you have lived is the main thing."

31. "Whatever one of us blames in another, each one will find in his own heart."

32. "To keep oneself safe does not mean to bury oneself."

33. "A man is as miserable as he thinks he is."

34.   "A man who suffers before it is necessary suffers more than is necessary."

35.   "No one is laughable who laughs at himself."

36.   "It's not because things are difficult that we dare not venture. It's because we dare not venture that they are difficult."

37.   "Life, if well lived, is long enough."

38.   "You are unfortunate in my judgment, for you have never been unfortunate. You have passed through life with no antagonist to face you; no one will know what you were capable of, not even you yourself.'"

39.   "Fate leads the willing and drags along the reluctant."

40.   "It is not the man who has too little, but the man who craves more, that is poor."

41.   "Despise Death, Yield not to adversity, trust not to prosperity, have scorn and contempt for the gifts of chance"

42.   "A brave man can live and die in defiance of death."

43.   "You will know you are wise when you are Joyful, Calm, Happy, and Unshaken."

44.   "Life is like a play: it's not the length, but the excellence of the acting that matters."

45.   "Until we have begun to go without them, we fail to realize how unnecessary many things are. We've been using

them not because we needed them but because we had them."

46. "True happiness is to enjoy the present, without anxious dependence upon the future, not to amuse ourselves with either hopes or fears but to rest satisfied with what we have, which is sufficient, for he that is so wants nothing. The greatest blessings of mankind are within us and within our reach. A wise man is content with his lot, whatever it may be, without wishing for what he has not."

47. "Until we have begun to go without them, we fail to realize how unnecessary many things are. We've been using them not because we needed them but because we had them."

48. "It is not the man who has too little that is poor, but the one who hankers after more."

49. "The point is, not how long you live, but how nobly you live."

50. "That which Fortune has not given, she cannot take away."

51. "Let Nature deal with matter, which is her own, as she pleases; let us be cheerful and brave in the face of everything, reflecting that it is nothing of our own that perishes."

52. "Virtue is nothing else than right reason."

53. "It is the power of the mind to be unconquerable."

54. "For what prevents us from saying that the happy life is to have a mind that is free, lofty, fearless and steadfast a mind that is placed beyond the reach of fear, beyond the reach

of desire, that counts virtue the only good, baseness the only evil, and all else but a worthless mass of things, which come and go without increasing or diminishing the highest good, and neither subtract any part from the happy life nor add any part to it?

A man thus grounded must, whether he wills or not, necessarily be attended by constant cheerfulness and a joy that is deep and issues from deep within, since he finds delight in his own resources, and desires no joys greater than his inner joys."

55. "Remember that all we have is "on loan" from Fortune, which can reclaim it without our permission—indeed, without even advance notice. Thus, we should love all our dear ones, but always with the thought that we have no promise that we may keep them forever—nay, no promise even that we may keep them for long."

56. "But is life really worth so much? Let us examine this; it's a different inquiry. We will offer no solace for so desolate a prison house; we will encourage no one to endure the overlordship of butchers. We shall rather show that in every kind of slavery, the road of freedom lies open. I will say to the man to whom it befell to have a king shoot arrows at his dear ones [Prexaspes], and to him whose master makes fathers banquet on their sons' guts [Harpagus]: 'What are you groaning for, fool?... Everywhere you look you find an end to your sufferings. You see that steep drop off? It leads down to freedom. You see that ocean, that river, that well? Freedom lies at its bottom. You see that short, shriveled, bare tree? Freedom hangs from it.... You ask, what is the path to freedom? Any vein in your body."

57. "Love sometimes injures. Friendship always benefits, after friendship is formed you must trust, but before that you must judge."

58. "My advice is really this: what we hear the philosophers saying and what we find in their writings should be applied in our pursuit of the happy life. We should hunt out the helpful pieces of teaching, and the spirited and noble minded sayings which are capable of immediate practical application—not far fetched or archaic expressions or extravagant metaphors and figures of speech—and learn them so well that words become works. No one to my mind lets humanity down quite so much as those who study philosophy as if it were a sort of commercial skill and then proceed to live in a quite different manner from the way they tell other people to live."

59. "Luck is what happens when preparation meets opportunity."

60. "All cruelty springs from weakness."

61. "Religion is regarded by the common people as true, by the wise as false, and by rulers as useful."

62. "Difficulties strengthen the mind, as labor does the body."

63. "Non est ad astra mollis e terris via" "There is no easy way from the earth to the stars"

64. "As is a tale, so is life: not how long it is, but how good it is, is what matters."

65.   "He suffers more than necessary, who suffers before it is necessary."

66.   "Only time can heal what reason cannot."

67.   "Associate with people who are likely to improve you."

68.   "The sun also shines on the wicked."

69.   "Leisure without books is death, and burial of a man alive."

70.   "Nothing is more honorable than a grateful heart."

71.   "errare humanum est, sed perseverare diabolicum: 'to err is human, but to persist (in the mistake) is diabolical."

72.   "Most men alternate in wretchedness between the fear of the hardships of life, and the fear of death"

73.   " So Let us Clothe ourselves with a Heroes Courage, and remove ourselves from the common opinions of men."

74.   "Many men have endured separate trials: Mucius by fire, Sextius by crucifixion, Socrates by poison, and Cato by the sword, so let us too overcome something, and be included among the Greats of History "

75.   "Men do not care how nobly they live, but only how long, although it is within the reach of every man to live nobly, but within no man's power to live long."

76.   "There are a few men whom slavery holds fast, but there are many more who hold fast to slavery."

77. "A good man will not waste himself upon mean and discreditable work or be busy merely for the sake of being busy."

78. "Accordingly, look about you for the opportunity; if you see it, grasp it, and with all your energy and with all your strength devote yourself to this task."

79. "If you wish,' said he, 'to make Pythocles rich, do not add to his store of money, but subtract from his desires."

80. "Prove your words by your deeds."

81. "Let us become intimate with poverty, so that Fortune may not catch us off our guard. We shall be rich with all the more comfort, if we once learn how far poverty is from being a burden."

82. "Change the age in which you live, and you have too much. But in every age, what is enough remains the same. "

83. "If anything forbids you to live nobly, nothing forbids you to die nobly."

84. "If you wish to have leisure for your mind, either be a poor man, or resemble a poor man. Study cannot be helpful unless you take pains to live simply; and living simply is voluntary poverty."

85. "If you live according to nature, you will never be poor; if you live according to opinion, you will never be rich."

86. "A happy life is reached when our wisdom is brought to completion, but that life is at least endurable even when our

wisdom is only begun."

87. "The fool's life is empty of gratitude and full of fears; its course lies wholly toward the future."

88. "Next, we must follow the old adage and avoid three things with special care: hatred, jealousy, and scorn."

89. "There are more things likely to frighten us than there are to crush us; we suffer more often in imagination than in reality."

90. "When a man has said: 'I have lived!', every morning he arises he receives a bonus."

91. "Happy is the man who can make others better, not merely when he is in their company, but even when he is in their thoughts!"

92. "Nothing is needed by the fool, for he does not understand how to use anything, but he is in want of everything"

93. "Hope and fear, dissimilar as they are, keep step together; fear follows hope."

94. "Pleasure, unless it has been kept within bounds, tends to rush headlong into the abyss of sorrow."

95. "The primary indication, to my thinking, of a well ordered mind is a man's ability to remain in one place and linger in his own company."

96. "No man can have a peaceful life who thinks too much about lengthening it. "

97. "Most men ebb and flow in wretchedness between the fear of death and the hardships of life; they are unwilling to live, and yet they do not know how to die. "

98. "Cease to hope,' he says, 'and you will cease to fear."

99. "If you seek joy in the midst of cares, these objects for which you strive so eagerly as if they would give you happiness and pleasure, are merely causes of grief."

100. "How can a man learn, in the struggle against his vices, an amount that is enough, if the time which he gives to learning is only the amount left over from his vices?"

101. "Before I became old I tried to live well; now that I am old, I shall try to die well; but dying well means dying gladly."

102. "We must make ready for death before we make ready for life."

103. "If you really want to escape the things that harass you, what you're needing is not to be in a different place but to be a different person."

104. "Enjoy present pleasures in such a way as not to injure future ones."

105. "If you live in harmony with nature you will never be poor; if you live according what others think, you will never be rich."

106. "Regard [a friend] as loyal, and you will make him loyal."

107. "It is not the man who has too little that is poor, but the one who hankers after more."

108. "Limiting one's desires actually helps to cure one of fear. 'Cease to hope ... and you will cease to fear.' ... Widely different [as fear and hope] are, the two of them march in unison like a prisoner and the escort he is handcuffed to. Fear keeps pace with hope ... both belong to a mind in suspense, to a mind in a state of anxiety through looking into the future. Both are mainly due to projecting our thoughts far ahead of us instead of adapting ourselves to the present."

109. "Nothing is burdensome if taken lightly, and nothing need arouse one's irritation so long as one doesn't make it bigger than it is by getting irritated."

110. "But when you are looking on anyone as a friend when you do not trust him as you trust yourself, you are making a grave mistake, and have failed to grasp sufficiently the full force of true friendship."

111. "What man can you show me who places any value on his time, who reckons the worth of each day, who understands that he is dying daily? For we are mistaken when we look forward to death; the major portion of death has already passed, Whatever years be behind us are in death's hands."

112. "Withdraw into yourself, as far as you can. Associate with those who will make a better man of you. Welcome those whom you yourself can improve. The process is mutual; for men learn while they teach."

113. "You should ... live in such a way that there is nothing

which you could not as easily tell your enemy as keep to yourself."

114. "Of this one thing make sure against your dying day that your faults die before you do."

115. "To win true freedom you must be a slave to philosophy."

116. "Philosophy calls for simple living, not for doing penance, and the simple way of life need not be a crude one."

117. "For many men, the acquisition of wealth does not end their troubles, it only changes them"

118. "There is no enjoying the possession of anything valuable unless one has someone to share it with"

119. "To be everywhere is to be nowhere."

120. "What really ruins our character is the fact that none of us looks back over his life."

121. "I have learned to be a friend to myself Great improvement this indeed Such a one can never be said to be alone for know that he who is a friend to himself is a friend to all mankind"

122. "A woman is not beautiful when her ankle or arm wins compliments, but when her total appearance diverts admiration from the individual parts of her body."

123. "Each day acquire something that will fortify you against poverty, against death, indeed against other

misfortunes as well; and after you have run over many thoughts, select one to be thoroughly digested that day."

124.   "What fortune has made yours is not your own."

125.   "Wild animals run from the dangers they actually see, and once they have escaped them worry no more. We however are tormented alike by what is past and what is to come. A number of our blessings do us harm, for memory brings back the agony of fear while foresight brings it on prematurely. No one confines his unhappiness to the present."

126.   "Because thou writest me often, I thank thee … Never do I receive a letter from thee, but immediately we are together."

127.   "People who know no self restraint lead stormy and disordered lives, passing their time in a state of fear commensurate with the injuries they do to others, never able to relax."

128.   "Let us say what we feel, and feel what we say; let speech harmonize with life."

129.   "The difficulty comes from our lack of confidence."

130.   "As it is with a play, so it is with life   what matters is not how long the acting lasts, but how good it is."

131.   "For the only safe harbour in this life's tossing, troubled sea is to refuse to be bothered about what the future will bring and to stand ready and confident, squaring the breast to take without skulking or flinching whatever fortune hurls at us."

132. "It is the power of the mind to be unconquerable."

133. "What is the point of dragging up sufferings that are over, of being miserable now, because you were miserable then?"

134. "True happiness is to enjoy the present, without anxious dependence upon the future, not to amuse ourselves with either hopes or fears but to rest satisfied with what we have, which is sufficient, for he that is so wants nothing."

135. "Set aside a certain number of days during which you shall be content with the scantiest and cheapest fare, with coarse and rough dress, saying to yourself the while, 'Is this the condition that I feared?"

136. "If a person doesn't know to which port they sail, no wind is favourable."

137. "There is only one way to happiness and that is to cease worrying about things which are beyond the power of our will."

138. "Nothing, to my way of thinking, is a better proof of a well ordered mind than a man's ability to stop just where he is and pass some time in his own company."

139. "Choose someone whose way of life as well as words, and whose very face as mirroring the character that lies behind it, have won your approval. Be always pointing him out to yourself either as your guardian or as your model. This is a need, in my view, for someone as a standard against which our characters can measure themselves. Without a ruler to do it against you won't make the crooked straight."

140. "We must give up many things to which we are addicted, considering them to be good. Otherwise, courage will vanish, which should continually test itself. Greatness of soul will be lost, which can't stand out unless it disdains as petty what the mob regards as most desirable."

141. "The greatest portion of peace of mind is doing nothing wrong. Those who lack self control live disoriented and disturbed lives."

142. Whoever has nothing to hope, let him despair of nothing.

143. "Wherever there is a human being, there is an opportunity for a kindness."

The quotes from Seneca are now over. Let's now hear about Epictetus's version of stoicism through 33 stoic quotes.

Famous Stoicism Quotes from Epictetus

Before we start the quotes, here is a quick introduction about who is Epictetus..
Epictetus was a Greek stoic philosopher. He was born as a slave at Hierapolis Phrygia which is Turkey in the present day.

Epictetus taught that philosophy is a way of life and not just a theory to discipline people. He has the belief that all external happenings are beyond our control and we should accept it calmly whatever happens. However, people are responsible for their own actions, which they can examine and control through rigorous discipline.

It is known that he lived a long life alone and in simplicity, it is also said that he had very few possessions. His student Arrian was the most people that studied under him describe Epictetus as a powerful speaker who could induce his listener to feel just what he wanted a person to feel. He has a great influence on the modern world especially in military, religion, and to other notable people as well in the ancient and modern world.

Although there were no surviving writing of Epictetus that are available, thanks to his student Arrian because of him we have a little glimpse of how great Epictetus is! Arrian transcribed and compiled the discourses of his teacher Epictetus which became the reference of who Epictetus was.

Make sure to be ready, here are the stoicism quotes from Epictetus:

1. "How long are you going to wait before you demand the best for yourself?"

2. "Don't seek for everything to happen as you wish it would, but rather wish that everything happens as it actually will—then your life will flow well."

3. "First say to yourself what you would be; and then do what you have to do."

4. "Curb your desire—don't set your heart on so many things and you will get what you need."

5. "Difficulties are things that show a person what they are."

6. "We should always be asking ourselves: "Is this something that is, or is not, in my control?"

7. "Define for me now what the "indifferents" are. Whatever things we cannot control. Tell me the upshot. They are nothing to me."

8. "It's something like going on an ocean voyage. What can I do? Pick the captain, the boat, the date, and the best time to sail. But then a storm hits... What are my options? I do the only thing I am in a position to do, drown—but fearlessly, without bawling or crying out to God, because I know that what is born must also die."

9. Take a lyre player: he's relaxed when he performs alone, but put him in front of an audience, and it's a different story, no matter how beautiful his voice or how well he plays the instrument. Why? Because he not only wants to perform well, he wants to be well received—and the latter lies outside his control.

10. ."Keep silence for the most part, and speak only when you must, and then briefly."

11. "Is freedom anything else than the right to live as we wish? Nothing else."

12. "No greater thing is created suddenly, any more than a bunch of grapes or a fig. If you tell me that you desire a fig, I answer you that there must be time. Let it first blossom, then bear fruit, then ripen."

13. "That's why the philosophers warn us not to be satisfied with mere learning, but to add practice and then training. For as time passes we forget what we learned and end up doing the opposite, and hold opinions the opposite of what we should."

14. "Don't explain your philosophy. Embody it."

15. "The chief task in life is simply this: to identify and separate matters so that I can say clearly to myself which are externals not under my control, and which have to do with the choices I actually control. Where then do I look for good and evil? Not to uncontrollable externals, but within myself to the choices that are my own..."

16. "If anyone tells you that a certain person speaks ill of you, do not make excuses about what is said of you but answer, 'He was ignorant of my other faults, else he would have not mentioned these alone.'"

17. You know yourself what you are worth in your own eyes; and at what price you will sell yourself. For men sell themselves at various prices. This is why, when Florus was deliberating whether he should appear at Nero's shows, taking part in the

performance himself, Agrippinus replied, 'Appear by all means.' And when Florus inquired, 'But why do not you appear?' he answered, 'Because I do not even consider the question.' For the man who has once stooped to consider such questions, and to reckon up the value of external things, is not far from forgetting what manner of man he is."

18. "What really frightens and dismays us is not external events themselves, but the way in which we think about them. It is not things that disturb us, but our interpretation of their significance."

19. "Remember to act always as if you were at a symposium. When the food or drink comes around, reach out and take some politely; if it passes you by don't try pulling it back. And if it has not reached you yet, don't let your desire run ahead of you, be patient until your turn comes. Adopt a similar attitude with regard to children, wife, wealth and status, and in time, you will be entitled to dine with the gods. Go further and decline these goods even when they are on offer and you will have a share in the gods' power as well as their company. That is how Diogenes, Heraclitus and philosophers like them came to be called, and considered, divine."

20. "If you want to make progress, put up with being perceived as ignorant or naive in worldly matters, don't aspire to a reputation for sagacity. If you do impress others as somebody, don't altogether believe it. You have to realize, it isn't easy to keep your will in agreement with nature, as well as externals. Caring about the one inevitably means you are going to shortchange the other."

21. "The first and most important field of philosophy is the application of principles such as "Do not lie." Next come the

proofs, such as why we should not lie. The third field supports and articulates the proofs, by asking, for example, "How does this prove it? What exactly is a proof, what is logical inference, what is contradiction, what is truth, what is falsehood?" Thus, the third field is necessary because of the second, and the second because of the first. The most important, though, the one that should occupy most of our time, is the first. But we do just the opposite. We are preoccupied with the third field and give that all our attention, passing the first by altogether. The result is that we lie but have no difficulty proving why we shouldn't."

22. "For in this Case, we are not to give Credit to the Many, who say, that none ought to be educated but the Free; but rather to the Philosophers, who say, that the Well educated alone are free."

23. "What upsets people is not things themselves, but their judgments about these things."

24. "It is impossible that happiness, and yearning for what is not present, should ever be united."

25. "Man is not worried by real problems so much as by his imagined anxieties about real problems."

26. "Man is disturbed not by things, but by the views he takes of them."

27. "If, therefore, any be unhappy, let him remember that he is unhappy by reason of himself alone."

28. Wealth consists not in having great possessions, but in having few wants.

29.   Don't just say you have read books. Show that through them you have learned to think better, to be a more discriminating and reflective person. Books are the training weights of the mind. They are very helpful, but it would be a bad mistake to suppose that one has made progress simply by having internalized their contents.

30.   "What does Socrates say? 'Just as one person delights in improving his farm, and another his horse, so I delight in attending to my own improvement day by day.'"

31.   "Now is the time to get serious about living your ideals. How long can you afford to put off who you really want to be? Your nobler self cannot wait any longer. Put your principles into practice   now. Stop the excuses and the procrastination. This is your life! [...] Decide to be extraordinary and do what you need to do now."

32.   "It is impossible for a man to learn what he thinks he already knows."

33.   "It is more necessary for the soul to be cured than the body; for it is better to die than to live badly."

The quotes from Epictetus are now over. Let's now hear about Zeno's version of stoicism through 6 stoic quotes.

Famous Stoicism Quotes from Zeno of Citium

Before we start the quotes, here is a quick introduction about who is Zeno of Citium.

Zeno of Citium is a Greek philosopher who was the founder of stoic school of Philosophy and was considered the founder of stoicism. He was born in the year 334 BCE in Citium, Cyprus. He was a Hellenistic thinker of Phoenician descent.

At around 300 BCE he founded the Stoic school of philosophy, which he taught in Athens it is based on moral ideas of the Cynics which has a great emphasis on goodness and peace of mind gained from living a life of Virtue in accordance with nature.

He was a wealthy man but despite of that he is described as humble. He always looked haggard despite of his riches. It is said that his interest in philosophy started when he consulted the oracle to know what he should do to attain the best life, and that the god' response that he should take on the complexion of the dead because of this he studied ancient authors.

He died in the year 262 BC, when he suddenly collapsed upon leaving the school. During his lifetime he had received a lot of award because of his works and achievements he was also given a golden crown and a tomb was built in honor of his moral influence on the youth of his era.

Let's start with a selection of the best 6 Stoicism Quotes from the founder of Stoicism :

1. "Happiness is a good flow of life."

2. "No evil is honorable, but death is honorable, therefore death is not evil."

3. "A bad feeling is a commotion of the mind repugnant to reason, and against nature."

4. "The cold of winter and the ceaseless rain
Come powerless against him: weak the dart
Of the fierce summer sun or racking pain
To bend that iron frame. He stands apart
Unspoiled by public feast and jollity:
Patient, unwearied night and day doth he
Cling to his studies of philosophy."

5.
"Here lies great Zeno, dear to Citium,
who scaled high Olympus,
though he piled not Pelion on Ossa,
nor toiled at the labours of Heracles,
but this was the path he found out to the stars
   the way of temperance alone."

6.
"Thou madest self sufficiency thy rule,
Eschewing haughty wealth, O godlike Zeno,
With aspect grave and hoary brow serene.
A manly doctrine thine: and by thy prudence
With much toil thou didst found a great new school,
Chaste parent of unfearing liberty.
And if thy native country was Phoenicia,
What need to slight thee? came not Cadmus thence,
Who gave to Greece her books and art of writing?"

The quotes from Zeno of Citium are now over. Let's now hear about various stoics' version of stoicism through 36 stoic quotes.

33 Various Quotes from Different Stoics

Make sure to be ready, here are the stoicism quotes from various stoics such as Shakespeare, Cato, Ryan Holiday, William Barclay and many more:

Let's start now:

1. "Endurance is not just the ability to bear a hard thing, but to turn it into glory." William Barclay

2. "Death remembered should be like a mirror, Who tells us life's but breath, to trust it error." William Shakespeare

3. "The stoicism that comes of endurance has something of death in it." Mary Catherwood

4. "Progress daily in your own uncertainty. Live in awareness of the questions." Bremer Acosta

5. "The average man is a conformist, accepting miseries and disasters with the stoicism of a cow standing in the rain." Colin Wilson

6. "What's the good of being stoical if nobody notices?" Mason Cooley

7. "Some of the best things that have ever happened to us wouldn't have happened to us, if it weren't for some of the worst things that have ever happened to us." Mokokoma Mokhonoana

8.   "The critics could never mortify me out of heart, because I love poetry for its own sake, and, tho' with no stoicism and some ambition, care more for my poems than for my poetic reputation."   Elizabeth Barrett Browning

9.   "Stoicism and silence does not serve us nor our communities, only the forces of things as they are."   Audre Lorde

10.   "The basic philosophy of stoicism is that you have nothing real external to your own consciousness, that the only thing real is in fact your consciousness."   Roger Avary

11.   "Once we accept our limits, we go beyond them".   Albert Einstein

12.   "When you give your items away, don't keep the excess of your pride."   Bremer Acosta

13.   Stoicism is the wisdom of madness and cynicism the madness of wisdom.   Bergen Evans

14.   "Warriors should suffer their pain silently."   Erin Hunter

15.   "What man actually needs is not a tensionless state but rather the striving and struggling for some goal worthy of him."   Viktor Frank

16.   "Stoicism is about the domestication of emotions, not their elimination."   Nassim Nicholas Taleb

17.   "I begin to speak only when I'm certain what I'll say isn't better left unsaid."   Cato

18. "What man actually needs is not a tensionless state but rather the striving and struggling for some goal worthy of him." Viktor Frankl

19. "When we are no longer able to change a situation, we are challenged to change ourselves."   Viktor Frankl

20. "Sometimes in life we must fight not only without fear, but also without hope. " Alessandro Pertini

21. "Feeling too much is a hell of a lot better than feeling nothing."   Nora Roberts

22. "Imagine smiling after a slap in the face. Then think of doing it twenty four hours a day."   Markus Zusak, "The Book Thief".

23. "Strength is the ability to maintain a hold of oneself. It's being the person who never gets mad, who cannot be rattled, because they are in control of their passions—rather than controlled by their passions."   Ryan Holiday

24. "Don't you deserve to flourish? Wouldn't you like to be great of soul, filled with confidence, and invincible to external events? ... Then practice your philosophy."   Ryan Holiday

25. "Having an end in mind is no guarantee that you'll reach it—no Stoic would tolerate that assumption—but not having an end in mind is a guarantee you won't."   Ryan Holiday

26. "Strength is the ability to maintain a hold of oneself. It's being the person who never gets mad, who cannot be rattled,

because they are in control of their passions—rather than controlled by their passions." Ryan Holiday

27. "Don't you deserve to flourish? Wouldn't you like to be great of soul, filled with confidence, and invincible to external events? ... Then practice your philosophy." Ryan Holiday

28. "Having an end in mind is no guarantee that you'll reach it—no Stoic would tolerate that assumption—but not having an end in mind is a guarantee you won't." Ryan Holiday

29. "Our ambition should not be to win, then, but to play with our full effort." Ryan Holiday

30. "Focus on the moment, not the monsters that may or may not be up ahead." Ryan Holiday, The Obstacle Is The Way

31. "It's okay to be discouraged. It's not okay to quit. To know you want to quit but to plant your feet and keep inching closer until you take the impenetrable fortress you've decided to lay siege to in your own life—that's persistence." Ryan Holiday, The Obstacle Is The Way

32. "You know what's better than building things up in your imagination? Building things up in real life." Ryan Holiday, The Obstacle Is The Way

33. "Your potential, the absolute best you're capable of—that's the metric to measure yourself against. Your standards are. Winning is not enough. People can get lucky and win. People can be assholes and win. Anyone can win. But not

everyone is the best possible version of themselves." Ryan Holiday, Ego Is the Enemy

The reading of 33 Quotes from various Stoics are now over.

Next, we are going to explore the most mindful quotes and Spiritual and philosophical excerpt from the stoic school

Spiritual and philosophical quotes of stoic school

Now listen carefully we are going to start the quotes of the ancient stoic schools:
Hatred is not only a vice, but a vice which goes point blank against Nature.
Hatred divides instead of joining and frustrates God's will in human society.
One man is born to help another.
Hatred makes us destroy one another.
Love unites hatred separates.
Love is beneficial hatred is destructive.
Love succors even strangers, hatred destroys the most intimate friendship.
Love fills all hearts with joy, hatred ruins all those who possess it.
Nature is bountiful, hatred is pernicious.
It is not hatred, but mutual love, that holds all mankind together.

What is God?
The Mind of the universe.
What is He?
All that you see, and all that you don't see.
Guide and guardian of the universe,
Soul and spirit of the world,
Builder and master of so great a work
to Him all names belong.
Would you call Him Destiny?
You will not err.
Cause of causes, all things depend on Him.
Would you rather say Providence?

This will be right.
By His plan the world is guided safely through its motions.
Or Nature?

This title does Him no wrong.
Of Him are all things born, and in Him all things live.
Or Universe?
You are not mistaken.
He is all that we see,
wholly present in every part,
sustaining this entire creation.
If we had understanding,
Would we ever cease chanting and blessing the Divine Power,
both openly and in secret?

Whether digging or ploughing or eating, should we not sing a hymn to God?
Great is God, for He has given us the instruments to till the ground ...
He has given us hands, the power of digestion, and the wisdom of the body that controls the breath.
Great is God, for He has given us a mind to apprehend these things and to duly use them!

I am old and lame   what else can I do but sing to God?
Were I nightingale, I should do after the manner of a nightingale.
Were I a swan, I should do after the manner of a swan.
But now, since I am a reasonable man, I must sing to God: this is my work.
I will do it; I will not desert my post ...
And I call upon you to join this self   same hymn.

The Philosophers say that there is a God, and that His Will directs the Universe ... But the more important lesson is to discover God's nature. Upon discovering that nature, a man would please God by making his own nature like unto God's. If the Divine is faithful, he must also be faithful; if free, he must also be free; if beneficent, he must also be beneficent; if magnanimous, he must also be magnanimous. Thus to make God's nature one's own, a man must imitate Him in every thought, word, and deed.
Show me a Man of God.
Show me a man modeled after the doctrines that are ever upon his lips.
Show me a man who is hard pressed and happy,
In danger and happy,
On his death bed and happy,
in exile and happy,
In evil report and happy.
Show him to me.
I ask again.
So help me, Heaven,
I long to see one Man of God!
And if you cannot show me one fully realized, let me see one in whom the process is at work or one whose bent is in that direction.
Do me that favor!
Grudge it not to an old man, to behold such wonder.
Do you think I wish to see the Zeus or Athena of Phidias, sparkling with ivory and gold?

No. Show me one of you, a human soul, longing to be of one with God.
You have seen a hand, a foot, or perhaps a head severed from its body and lying some distance away. Such is the state a man brings himself to as far as he is able when he refuses to

accept what befalls him, breaks away from helping others, or when he pursues self seeking action. He becomes an outcast from the unity of Nature; though born of it, his own hand has cut him from it. Yet here is the beautiful proviso: it lies within everyone's power to join Nature once again. God has not granted such favor to any other part of creation: once you have been separated, once you have been cleft asunder, He will, at any moment, allow you to return.

Universe, all that is in tune with you is also in tune with me. Every note of your harmony resonates in my innermost being. For me, nothing is early and nothing is late if it is timely for you. O Nature, all that your seasons bring is fruit for me. From thee comes all things; in thee do all things live and grow; and to thee do all things return. "Dear City of God" is our cry, even though the poets say, "Dear City of the King."
Waste no more time talking about great souls and how they should he. Be one yourself!

Remember that the Hidden Power within us pulls the strings; there is the guiding force, there is the life, there, one might say, is the man himself Never think of yourself as a mere body with its various appendages; the body is like the ax of a carpenter: dare we think that the ax is the carpenter himself? Without this Inner Cause, which dictates both action and inaction, the body is of no more use than the weaver's shuttle without a weaver, the writer's pen without a writer, or the coachman's whip without a horse and carriage.

Honor the highest thing in the Universe; it is the power on which all things depend; it is the light by which all of life is guided. Honor the highest within yourself; for it, too, is the power on which all things depend, and the light by which all life is guided.

Dig within. Within is the well spring of Good; and it is always ready to bubble up, if you just dig.

It is possible to live out your whole life in perfect contentment, even though the whole world deafens you with its roar and wild beasts tear apart your body like a lump of clay. For nothing can shake a steady mind out of its peaceful repose; nothing can bar it from correct judgment, nor defeat its readiness to see the benefit that all things bring.

As Marcus, I have Rome; as a human being, I have the Universe.

Men may block your path, but never let them obstruct you from right action, never let them destroy the feeling of charity you have toward them. You must be firm in both: steadfast in judgment and action, kind to those who do you harm. To lose your temper with them is no less a sign of weakness than one cowed into abandoning his proper course of action. In both cases, the post of duty has been deserted.

Constantly remind yourself, I am a member of the whole body of conscious things." If you think of yourself as a mere "part," then love for mankind will not well up in your heart; you will look for some reward in every act of kindness and miss the boon which the act itself is offering. Then all your work will be seen as a mere duty and not as the very portal connecting you with the Universe itself.

In a man's life, his time is but a moment, his being a mere flux, his senses a dim glimpse, his body food for the worms, and his soul a restless eddy ... the things of the body pass like a flowing stream; life is a brief sojourn, and one's mark in this world is soon forgotten.

It is time to realize that you are a member of the Universe, that you are born of Nature itself, and to know that a limit has been set to your time. Use every moment wisely, to perceive your inner refulgence, or it will be gone and nevermore within your reach.

At daybreak, when you loathe the idea of having to leave your bed, have this thought ready in your mind: I am rising for the work of man." Should I have misgivings about doing that for which I was born, and for the sake of which I came into this world? Is this the grand purpose of my existence to lie here snug and warm underneath my blanket? Certainly it feels more pleasant. Was it for pleasure that you were made, and not for work, nor for effort? Look at the plants, sparrows, ants, spiders, and bees, all working busily away, each doing its part in welding an orderly Universe. So who are you to go against the bidding of Nature? Who are you to refuse man his share of the work?

To live each day as though it were your last never flustered, never lazy, never a false word herein lies the perfection of character.

This book about stoic quotes is now over.

I encourage you to read this book from time to time when you have spare time before you rest or directly after you woke up in the first part of the day or whenever you need to.

Set aside the opportunity to read again to these quotations as they will propel you and lift your spirit up.

Lastly, if you enjoyed this book I ask that you please take the time to review it on Audible.com. Your honest feedback would be greatly appreciated.
Thank you.

Now, I would like to share with you a free sneak peek to another one of my books that I think you will really enjoy. The book is called "Mindfulness Meditation: A Practical Guide for Beginners" Published by Barrie Muesse Scott and Mark Davenport. It's an Introduction to Learn Meditation and Become Mindful Guided Meditation, Self Hypnosis, Subliminal Affirmations, Stress Relief & Relaxation.

Enjoy!

This book is all about using the power of your thoughts to be mindful and bring peace, purpose, and happiness to your life.

Drawing upon the rich tradition of Buddhism, mindfulness meditation is all about using your thoughts to be present in the moment and crafting the world that you want to live in. If you want to be more present in your daily life, this book is for you. If you want to heal and cope with chronic diseases, this book is for you. If you want to just sleep better or deal with your depression, then this book is definitely for you. Mindfulness meditation has been shown to have extraordinary effects on your life from your mental to physical health. This book will show you how to tap into the beautiful power of mindfulness meditation no matter if you are Buddhist or not.

The following chapters will discuss everything you need to know about embracing mindfulness meditation in your day-to-day life. However, an important distinction between mindfulness and meditation needs to be made before we proceed. Oftentimes, you see mindfulness and meditation used together. Other times, you may see mindfulness and meditations used interchangeably. Meditation is the more general term that refers to the practice of fine-tuning your mind through various mental exercises. Mindfulness is a form of meditation in which one focuses on being in the very moment compared to other types of meditation practices that may use chants or mantras. For the purposes of this book, it is important to note this distinction. Any meditation practice is great! However, this book will dwell on the importance of honing in on your breath with your mindfulness meditation practice.

Mindfulness Meditation: A Practical Guide For Beginners covers five chapters. In chapter 1, mindfulness meditation will be discussed thoroughly. How key concepts in mindfulness meditation relate to Buddhism, plus the benefits of mindfulness meditation, plus answers to frequently asked questions are included. The subject of chapter 2 is about how to practice mindfulness meditation. A practical guide about which positions are best and other best practices are highlighted. Chapter 3 explores more breathing and relaxation techniques that can be used to bolster your mindfulness meditation practice. The techniques in this chapter are able to help you vary your mindfulness meditation practice. Chapter 4 is dedicated to guided mindfulness meditation exercises that can help you as you begin your meditation practice. The scrips included will help you get started so you do not have to start your meditation practice from scratch. Chapter 5 is also dedicated to guided meditations, but the mindfulness meditation scripts in this chapter focus on guided meditations designed to heal various ailments.

This book about Mindfulness and Meditation will more than prepare you to begin your journey into mindfulness and meditation. There are a lot of famous people who practice mindfulness like Naomie Harris, Boris Johnson, Katy Perry, Richard Branson, and Anderson Cooper to name a few; thus, you are in great company.

Chapter 1: What is Mindfulness Meditation?

"To think in terms of either pessimism or optimism oversimplifies the truth. The problem is to see reality as it is." – Thích Nhất Hạnh

How many times have we been encouraged to see the cup half full instead of half-empty? Oftentimes in western society, the push to be optimistic and to think positive is drilled into us from a young age. However, if one is beginning to become more mindful, the transition to mindfulness may feel a little jarring as it is opposite of what feels comfortable. Imagine this. Instead of focusing just on the positive aspect of life, mindfulness encourages a realistic outlook on life that embraces the good and the bad, the positive and the negative and the neutral. And this is where our book begins, starting off by learning about this effective way of living that has been used successfully for centuries – mindfulness meditation.

Buddhist monks have been using the power of mindfulness for over 2, 500 years. Mindfulness is the act of allowing your brain to rest while observing the thoughts that come and go in your mind. Mindfulness meditation is different from actively thinking and using your creative mind. When you are being mindful, you focus on an object, scene or sound that is calm and then let your thoughts gently amble by in your mind. Being mindful is powerful because if you are always caught up into being busy and always thinking about your next step, mindfulness gives you a much-needed break and makes you reflect on your pattern of thoughts and actions. It is the exact opposite of the daily living experience of most people because instead of going, mindfulness encourages you to slow down the pace.

Mindfulness allows you to know your thoughts instead of trying to change them. Instead of being judgmental and unkind to yourself if you think something negative, mindfulness has no judgment value on your thoughts. Your thoughts are just there. When you are mindful, you are taking notes of your thoughts like a note-taker. When you are in a mindful state, you just pay attention to what your thoughts are doing but giving them the freedom to do what they want. Ultimately, the goal of mindfulness is to know your mind. Once you begin to know your mind, you can begin the next step which is to train your mind.

The beautiful thing about our minds is that they are malleable, and as a result, they are trainable. Our minds are able to change based on what one is thinking. If you think the world is a horrible place, you will operate from a place of fear and your actions will show that. If you think that the world is a wonderful place, you will operate from a place of reckless optimism without being able to be realistic about certain dangers you may find yourself in. Mindfulness helps you to know your thoughts and then begin to train your thoughts to become more in tune with your long-term goals. Mindfulness slows down the grind of your busy daily pace and gives you a different vantage point about patterns in your life. These patterns can be feelings that you have in certain situations or your reactions to how other people treat you. When you are being mindful, you may notice trends and patterns that you are constantly thinking. Are you always wanting more and more? Do you feel comfortable with the way things are? Whatever patterns you notice, mindfulness can help you pinpoint what types of things are causing you mental, anguish, conflict, or joy. Then after noticing these patterns, you can begin to shape it to how you would like to be by focusing on being more gracious, compassionate, and kind with your thoughts.

When you begin your practice, do not treat your mindfulness meditation practices as an obligatory item on your daily to-do list. When you meditate, you want to be present in the moment, not treating the practice as an aggressive measuring stick to how fast you can change or using your meditation practice as a form of escapism without being willing to change your ideals. The most important thing to remember before you begin is that you are training your mind to be at peace with how things are going in the world, no matter what is happening. Once you are able to be at peace in no matter what situation you find yourself in, then you are able to start to work on yourself to change your values. Mindfulness meditation is not a sprint; it is a marathon that you continually work on until you are finally able to free yourself from unsavory emotions that are clinging to you whether they are anger, agitation, negativity, self-image issues, unfair, hasty judgments, and biased opinions and ideals.

When you are training your mind to be more mindful, affirmations are great tools to use. Affirmations are very helpful, especially when you create them yourself. The thought process behind using affirmations is to use very direct language which influences your subconscious to help you get the outcome that you want to get. When you use affirmations, you want to first figure out what outcome it is that you want. Then create a short sentence with an active word. Make sure the sentence is in the present tense. For example, if you want to feel calmer and not be so anxiety-ridden, you can create an affirmation to help. You will start with the outcome of being calmer and make that into a statement using the present tense. Thus, the affirmation would be 'I am more calm.' By using the present tense, you are affirming the future outcome. When the affirmation is created, you can say it during your meditation time and throughout the day. When you couple this practice of saying affirmations with your mindfulness meditation session, they work doubly together to help you get the outcome that you want to get. For example, you hear the term think positive all the time. It is because positive thinking can help shape your future to where you have a positive future. However, if you think negative oftentimes a reality reflects your thoughts. Our thoughts influence our subconscious which in turn can determine our reality.

Mindfulness meditation helps you shape your reality by taking the time to know your mind. Once you know your mind, you will be able to train it and ultimately free it from negative, debilitating thinking. Every step works together. Before you begin your mindfulness meditation practice, know that it is not going to be easy. It will be a journey, but if you are dedicated, you will see a difference in your life.

The History of Mindfulness Meditation

For Buddhists, nurturing mindfulness is the ultimate path to enlightenment. The point of Buddhism is to reach the highest truth by focusing on overcoming the limitations that your body has. Buddhists practice mindfulness by using four foundational truths of mindfulness. The four truths originate from a Buddhist sutta or sutra which is similar to a form of Buddhist scripture. The name of the sutta is called "The Discourse on the Establishing of Mindfulness" or the *Satipatthana sutta*. Please remember that the four establishments of mindfulness come from a very long and rich history. This book cannot possibly cover everything related to them, but hopes to serve as a general overview that can deepen your understanding of mindfulness meditation. The four truths are mindfulness of the body, mindfulness of feelings, mindfulness of consciousness and mindfulness of phenomena. Each foundation normally goes step-by-step in a flowing manner. You can go in and out of meditating upon each truth. They all work together. The first stop on the mindfulness journey is mindfulness of the body.

What is the one thing that you typically hear before beginning any form of meditation? The answer is watching your breath. Most meditation practices or guided meditations instruct you to begin by taking deep breaths in and exhaling deep breaths. Therefore, when you practice mindfulness, the first step is to think about mindfulness of your body. Initially, you'll want to start by being mindful of your breathing. Notice how deep or how shorts your breaths are when you start your meditation session. There are also different forms of body mindfulness you can focus on as well, such as mindfulness of eating or mindfulness of how you walk. These are some of the easiest mindfulness of the body to begin with, but we will focus on mindfulness of breathing since breathing is key to healing lots of ailments, physical and mental in your body.

Mindfulness of the body is just not about the positions your body is sitting in or how you breathe, eat and walk. Mindfulness of the body also involves a deeper understanding of how all your body parts work together. This includes how your leg connects to your thigh, how your ears function, or the power of body working throughout your body. Mindfulness of the body also seeks to understand some of the more unpleasant bodily functions such as urine or snot boogers or blood. The purpose of being mindful of your body is to reflect on how your body functions. You may ask, how do I try to be mindful of my body when I am meditating? An easy introductory way to do this is to imagine yourself greeting and thanking each body part for what it does. You can start at your feet and work your way up until you reach the top of your body.

The next foundation you should be concerned with when practicing mindfulness meditation is mindfulness of your feelings. A better way to explain mindfulness of your feelings is that this truth is concerned about being mindful of your neutral, painful, and pleasurable feelings. You can also reflect on how to be mindful of these feelings by using the senses of your touch, smell, hearing, seeing, taste, and your mind. In Buddhism, your mind is considered a sixth sense. It important to be mindful of these feelings because when you have painful feelings they can lead to fear and hatred. Too many neutral feelings can cause you to become disinterested and floated through life. When you are neutral about something, you are not concerned about it and as a result, it will not be important to you. Lastly, you have to be mindful of pleasurable feelings because too many pleasurable feelings can lead to lust and greed. It is important to be non-judgmental and only observe your thoughts, not acknowledge them when you meditate. The reason you do not want to acknowledge anything is that once you begin to acknowledge a thought as a neutral, painful or pleasurable feeling, you are in danger of attaching yourself to feelings that will prevent you from being enlightened. Thus, it is best to use mindfulness to observe when you are gaining feelings of neutrality, pleasure or painful so you know how to handle those feelings appropriately. When you practice mindfulness of feelings, you will still experience feelings.

Mindfulness of feelings does not mean that you do not feel. It only means that you are able to enjoy the feelings without going overboard to the point of the feelings cause you to become obsessed and overly attached to the thing that is causing the feeling, whether those feelings are good or bad. For example, if you love doughnuts and you find yourself obsessing over doughnuts, you can enjoy them so much that you want more and more doughnuts because of the pleasurable feeling that doughnuts give you. Eating too many doughnuts can cause issues your health like diabetes or chronic inflammation. All of these feelings started because of the seemingly innocent, yet pleasurable feeling of liking doughnuts. On the other side, if you are leery of a certain political leaning and it brings you immense pleasure, attaching yourself to that displeasure can quickly lead to hatred and biased feelings. However, if you are able to know your thoughts and know that this political leaning causes displeasure, you can work to be mindful that the political leaning is a trigger for you without attaching too much to that feeling to the point that it goes overboard. Likewise, if you feel neutral about a person, you can become so disinterested in them that you lose focus of the fact that they are human and worthy of respect. Hence, if they ever needed something, you would most likely overlook them or drag your feet to help them. So even feelings of neutrality can be dangerous. Once you become too attached to any type of feeling, the excess doting on the feeling prevents you from reaching enlightenment.

Thank you, this preview is now over.

I hope you enjoyed this preview of my book Mindfulness Meditation: A Practical Guide for Beginners - An Introduction to: Guided Meditation, Self Hypnosis, Subliminal Affirmations, Stress Relief & Relaxation. Learn to Meditate and Become Mindful" by Barrie Muesse Scott and Mark Davenport. Please make sure to check out the full book on Amazon.com

Thank you.

www.ingramcontent.com/pod-product-compliance
Lightning Source LLC
Chambersburg PA
CBHW030116100526
44591CB00009B/414